Culture Is The Bass

7 STEPS TO CREATING HIGH-PERFORMING TEAMS

Gerald J. Leonard

PPM ACADEMY PRESS

Discover the secret for taking your workplace culture from toxic stress to executing its best.

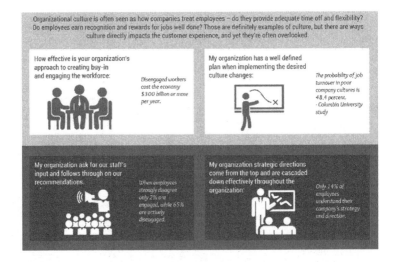

Take the Free 11 Most Common Workplace

Culture Mistakes Assessment

It takes less than 3 minutes to complete the assessment, and you will receive a free customized report of your results!

www.geraldjleonard.com/freegift

Special Bonus:

Receive $500 of tools, templates, videos, training, and processes that will increase your personal and business productivity today.

Go to

www.geraldjleonard.com/productivitybonuses

What people are saying about *Culture is the BASS*!

"Love the analogy/metaphor of music being compared to business. There are lots of similarities, as you show us. As a musician myself, I've often thought about how the two are similar - and how interesting it would be to create a speech, or in your case a book, around the topic."

Shep Hyken - Customer Service Expert, Keynote Speaker & New York Times and Wall Street Journal Best-Selling Author of Amaze Every Customer Every Time and The Amazement Revolution

"I've had the privilege of hearing Gerald Leonard speak half a dozen times, and his ideas are insightful, actionable, and energizing. I think the analogy with music works very well in this new book, and it adds a new perspective to looking at PPM."

Mitzi Perdue – Author of TOUGH MAN, TENDER CHICKEN, Business and Life Lessons from Frank Perdue

"What I love about this book is the analogy. Ever listened to just the tuba? Or second fiddles? It's really not that interesting. But when you put it together, it can move your soul... And professional musicians know that a good conductor brings a vision that transports the performance to a whole new level... but it's the underlying culture that forms the platform on which the conductor builds."

Stuart Easton - CEO of TransparentChoice

"Gerald, thanks for sharing this with us. I love the analogy of the orchestra to business, because just as the conductor needs to surround his / herself with the best players, so does the CEO or manager. Companies can't make beautiful "music" for their clients without the right people, in the right chairs. But you are also right to point out that every step in the process has to be right, both internally and customer-facing. Efficiency and creating an exceptional customer experience comes from planning and preparation, then execution. I'm sure companies, large and small, will benefit from reading this book... and so will their customers and bottom lines!"

Alan Berg – CSP Certified Speaking Professional®, Consultant, and Marketing Guru

"Gerald, thank you for the sneak peek at your newly released book. I enjoyed reading the metaphor of how a great culture is like an orchestra. You can't make beautiful music and enjoy harmony without a commitment from all to play their part. You must have the right leadership, and the right players, playing to their strengths. I work with companies all the time on building inclusive and high-performing workplace cultures, and your analogy is spot on as to what the end result should look like. Having a proper PPM process in place will certainly contribute to their achieving high-performance harmony. Thank you for sharing your expertise and strategies for how company cultures can be great, in sync, and high performing."

Shirley Davis, Ph.D., CSP, SPHR, SHRM-SCP President of SDS Global Enterprises, Inc.; Business Executive; Workforce Management Expert, Author of **Reinvent Yourself: Strategies for Achieving Success in Every Area of Your Life**

"Love the graphics. Excellent points. Culture is so difficult to define and affect. This approach really makes sense."

Serena E Sacks - CIO at Fulton County Schools

"Nice job, Gerald. Congrats on breathing life into a topic that is often uninteresting - where everyone is using the same tired ideas. I don't think one needs to be a musician to appreciate your metaphor. With that said, I think a musician will readily see the layers of content you have created with this very unique and interesting book."

Bill Cates, Hall of Fame Keynote Speaker, Author of Get More Referrals Now and Beyond Referrals

"Bravo, Gerald! While I played in a band in high school and college, I feel your analogy will work with anyone who listens to music. It has a universal appeal, and it's obvious how it can work well together and how it can be a disaster even with the best individual players. Keep charging forward!"

Buzz Walker - Global President, CEO, Board Member | Renewable, Internet Technology

"I love this - it is spot on with what an organization needs to have a successful culture. Every single company, community, family, and the organization have a culture, even if it is by accident. Having an on purpose culture is vital to the success of any group - and I believe Gerald J. Leonard has it down."

Brynne Tillman · Chief Learning Officer at PeopleLinx

"The analogy powerfully sketched the organization, collaboration, process alignment, and results delivery that PPM brings. I think that even someone new to project and portfolio management (and being a music enthusiast helps) can be able to wrap his/her arms around these concepts."

MaricarBurt Dilan · Calgary, Alberta

"Just as there are different levels of performance of orchestras, there are different levels of portfolio management success, and Gerald Leonard gives a fresh perspective through his case studies and multi-faceted experience. One of the biggest takeaways for me was thinking about the relationship between engagement and success."

Gabriela Cadena, PMP, CERT, ALB/ACB Project Management * Speaker * Creative Thinker

"Gerald, you created a masterpiece. Using music as the metaphor for culture opened up my mind, and it is so true in the business world. I never equated music and business, but I now see the direct correlation."

Darlene T. Carver, Co-author of THE MASTERS OF SUCCESS, along with Ken Blanchard, Jack Canfield, and John Christensen.

Gerald J. Leonard/PPM Academy Press
PO Box 984
Bay Minette, AL, 36507
http://developingaculturethatworks.com/

Printed in the United States

PROJECT MANAGER: John Peragine • info@osiris-papers.com

Ordering Information:
Quantity sales. Special discounts are available on quantity purchases by corporations, associations, and others. For details, contact the "Special Sales Department" at the address above.

Culture Is The Bass/ Gerald J. Leonard. —New Ed.
ISBN-13: 978-17340050-0-4

Table of Contents

DEDICATION

This book is dedicated to my son Kenon and daughter Peyton for loving me through my life's journey, and personal growth. They have helped me become the man I am today.

Also to my Mom and Dad, Lola J. Leonard and Willie C. Leonard, for without your love, compassion, and discipline, I would not know what a hardworking, loving, and compassionate family man is.

Finally, to my siblings, Deborah D. Leonard, Sharon L. Stevens, Wendell L. Leonard, the late Harold L. Leonard, and Carolyn Leonard for protecting me, guiding me, and putting up with me; I love you deeply.

"Culture eats strategy for breakfast."

—Peter Drucker

CHAPTER 1

DISCOVERING PROJECT PORTFOLIO MANAGEMENT, OR EVERYTHING I LEARNED PLAYING IN AN ORCHESTRA

For as long as I can remember, I have been a musician. I have played the bass, both upright and electric, throughout my youth and into adulthood. During these many years as a professional and classically trained musician, I learned more than just playing notes. I learned systems and how they work together.

Consider an orchestra for a minute. You can break them into four sections:
Strings
Winds
Brass
Percussion

These are all led by a conductor. Within each of these sections, there are smaller sections.
Strings- Violin I, Violin II, Viola, Cello, and Bass (my favorite).
Winds- Flute, Oboe, Clarinet, and Bassoon.

Brass- Trumpet, Trombone, Horn, and Tuba.

Percussion- Timpani, Snare, Marimba, etc. (there are many different instruments in this section).

Within these sections, you can break them down into even smaller categories:

Strings- Inner player and outer player (players share a stand and can read two different parts from the same sheet of music).

Winds- Flute (Piccolo, Alto, Bass Flutes), Oboe (English Horn), Bassoon (Contra), and Clarinet (there are many sizes of clarinet, all the way to Contra Bass).

Brass- Trumpets (Piccolo, and other sizes), Trombone (Bass), and Tuba (Euphonium).

Percussion- Like I said earlier percussionists must be the master of all types of instruments- the one rule is they must be struck. Did you know that a piano is considered a percussion instrument?

In each section, there is a hierarchy- usually, the first chair runs the section, and they usually have the second chair as a partner. If there were a president of an orchestra, it would be the concertmaster- or first chair violin. The conductor can be thought of as the CEO.

This is not meant as a music lesson, more of a structure you may not have considered, but one I will refer to in this book. Sometimes to understand a concept, whether new or old, you have to think outside your usual understanding and context. It forces your mind to focus and concentrate because it is new, innovative, and hopefully for the sake of this book, interesting.

Each concert that an orchestra prepares for is preceded by rehearsals, and this is the "production" of the piece to be performed. There are two parts to this process - orchestra rehearsal, and sectionals.

Think of the orchestra's seasonal concert series as your portfolio. Each concert in the series is a sub-portfolio, and each musical composition in a concert is synonymous to a project in the portfolio. Project Portfolio Management (PPM) is the decision process to determine which musical selection shall be included, categorized, prioritized and arranged in each concert and must be aligned with the Orchestra's seasonal theme, or strategic objective of the executive director and conductor.

The sectionals are split up, so my Bass section would be working on our part of the music - this is project management. We have a specific project - music preparation. We must then fit back into to larger orchestra, or the portfolio during the rehearsal.

What is universal within the sectionals and the regular orchestra rehearsal is what I will be referring to as culture.

The whole point of PPM is to establish a culture that allows a process that systematically aligns those differences into a cohesive, aligned (and prioritized) portfolio that yields better results for the investment of company resources.

Each section in an orchestra is different. Each instrument is played differently, and even the music is written differently for different types of instruments, but there has to be some cohesive glue that allows each instrument and section to play together. It is not good enough for the individual sections to perform flawlessly; they must perform within the larger orchestra. Each department within a company may have a flawless record of project management implementation, but if the culture is not there, it will not save an entire company. It is up to the conductor to make the sections play together within the context of the music to create a moving performance. It is up to a CEO to implement a culture that works and for the leadership team to make the company perform at its best and grow.

Why is PPM important?

Can you imagine going to a music performance, (any type will do) and the musicians are not playing together? Each of them is buried in their own musical performance with sound canceling headphones on. They are not in sync with either tempo or volume. Each of them playing every note perfectly. Does this sound like something you would want to spend an evening listening too?

Everyday companies fail to compete in the market and grow because of a poor project portfolio management culture. Without a culture that's driven by strong PPM processes, committed leadership team, and empirical data for decision-making, there can be no balance, harmony, or unified vision. Everyone would be buried in their own processes, but no one would be driving the company toward a unified goal. Even if the smaller systems are working, they are only cogs in a larger system, which will eventually break down.

Having a great sales team will get clients in the door, but if the team's delivery is slow and behind, the clients will lose faith. They may ask for a refund, not return in the future, or even worse: put a bad review on your favorite social media platform (i.e., Yelp, Twitter, Facebook, LinkedIn, Google+, etc.....).

What happens, in this case, is that there is a breakdown in the system - and the finger-pointing and blaming game begins, which does nothing to help resolve the overall issue.

The true value proposition of an effective PPM capability is that it enables an organization to achieve a data-driven decision-making process, engages senior leaders throughout the company, and creates a true competitive advantage that delivers a standard of excellence in strategy implementation and execution that consistently produces and exceeds stakeholder expectations and project outcomes by:

- Reducing risk
- Maximizing ROI
- Speeding realization of business value
- Driving effective organizational change
- Creating an organizational culture that works!

Different Music = Different Projects

An orchestra must be able to take on new projects every concert in the form of music. They have to be able to deliver quality music in a short amount of time. Often an orchestra only has a couple of weeks or days to prepare. They have to be able to play all types of music from many different genres and composers across centuries. Some of it is harder to perform and takes more individual practice and dedication. Because there is a process and a culture of excellence cultivated with a clear vision in place, they are able to deliver a quality concert consistently, no matter what type of music they are asked to perform.

In the same way, not every project is created equal. A large project may require some overtime hours to accomplish, while a small project may open the door for some free time that can be used to create additional value; think 3M or Google 20% employee innovation time.

A project management framework needs to be flexible, whether you're using a waterfall or agile process. It needs to be streamlined; allowing projects to be delivered consistently, but the idea is not just to focus on the process. The focus is on projects delivering business value as quickly and efficiently as possible, in alignment with the organization's strategic goals and objectives.

If an orchestra cannot play a versatile range of music, after a while, their performance will become predictable and stale. Audiences will turn elsewhere for their entertainment. There has to be a framework in place that allows new pieces to be practiced and performed.

Companies must design a framework for standardizing project management techniques within their strategic portfolio management environment. This is a step towards systematizing the format and content of project management information for all business and technical projects, whether they are internal or external to the organization. Hence, the beginning of building a strategy execution culture.

The benefits of implementing a standardized project management framework are as follows:

- Establishes and deploys a common set of management processes and templates.
- Increases knowledge sharing and best practices across projects.
- Creates reusable project management components that can reduce project start-up time, ensure timely project starts, and formal project ends.
- Improves communication.
- Includes consistently defined roles and responsibilities.
- Establishes a clear line of ownership for tasks and accountability by resources to execute task requirements.
- More efficient use of constrained resources.

- Improves monitoring of project status.
- Earlier detection of problems that may affect the project.
- Measurable improvements in the quality of project deliverables.
- Efficiencies and economies of scale due to consistency in project management and knowledge management practices.

It took many years, and I am sure many iterations for orchestras to come up with a structure that works; and for the most part, this structure and the expectations inherent in that structure are the same around the world. If I sit down with an orchestra in Memphis, Tennessee, or with an orchestra in Shanghai, the structure is predictable. There may be slight variations, but I know what is expected when I arrive.

1. I have an instrument in good working order.
2. I have my music.
3. If possible, I will have looked at the music beforehand and practiced.
4. I know that the conductor will play through the music and may stop in certain sections to improve the music. This is repeated until the time is done.
5. If I am in a sectional rehearsal, the structure is pretty much the same, but the section leader (first chair) is running the rehearsal.
6. If I am in a jazz combo rehearsal, it is the same.

And so on…

There is a standardization that has occurred over the entire industry that works. It is a culture that permeates all ensemble music. There are other industries, such as the food industry, that have standard modes of operation and structure, for safety reasons. Hospitals and health care systems also have these same type of regulations.

What I'm really talking about is an internal company standardization; a development of a culture that permeates each department and each project. The focus used to be, manage your schedule, manage your time, and manage your budget, but now it is about value creation. If you deliver on time, but you do not deliver value, then what good is it? Creating a culture that works helps define value within the entire organization.

In an orchestra, the determination of value is simple to conclude. At the end of a performance, an audience jumps to their feet and applauds because of the experience they've received.

To help you start the 7 STEPS TO CREATING HIGH-PERFORMING TEAMS journey, and it is a journey. Let's talk about the 11 most common mistakes organizations make in developing a culture that works. I've created a quick online assessment to help you determine where you are with these 11 mistakes and to give you a mental framework to use as you begin your journey. The 11 common mistakes are:

1. Taking the wrong approach to creating buy-in and engaging the workforce.
2. Poor or no plan to implement the desired culture.
3. Getting your staff's input, but not following through on any recommendations.
4. Too many directions from the top.
5. Not aligning culture changes with the organization's strategy and goals.
6. Lack of clear Roles and Responsibilities.
7. Leadership being inconsistent or Leadership, not setting an example of being the change they seek to make.
8. Taking on too much change, or Lack of capacity to absorb the change.
9. Not protecting your critical resources and people from the impact of too much change at once.
10. Not connecting emotionally with the team to help them navigate the change.
11. Poor stakeholder engagement and communication about the change throughout the transition process.

To take the 11 common mistakes, online assessment go to https://principlesofexecution.nsvey.net/ns/n/11CommonMistakes.aspx

Much of the change I'd like to implement starts with me. But that means I have to be there to follow-up, support, and guide along the way. Work shoulde to
shoulder.

CHAPTER 2

VISION

L et me begin by sharing a workable definition of what I mean by Vision.

A Dream or Mental Picture of what you want or want to become that is clear, and that drives you to achieve your goals and tasks to make it come true, persevering through obstacles and challenges to obtaining it.

When a conductor prepares for a performance, there are a couple of things they must work out first. The composer of any piece of music has a vision (at least an auditory one). Sometimes a conductor is lucky enough to have access to notes written by the composer about their vision, but that's not always the case. The vision for music usually involves emotion. The composer wants the audience to feel a certain way while experiencing the music. This may include a bit of an internal movie as the music may have a story it is portraying. A perfect example of this is Sergei Prokofiev's "Peter and the Wolf." In it, the listener is transported to a cold winter day in Russia in which a young boy is hunting a wolf. Along the way, he meets different animals, with each creature having a solo that is played by different instruments. It is easy to identify the different characters in the piece. This was his vision, and he pulled it off brilliantly.

Therefore, the conductor understands the vision of the composer. Now he or she must make a decision; what is their vision of the piece? How do they want to perform the piece? How will they interpret dots and lines on a page?

They must be prepared to share this vision with the orchestra using conducting, verbal, and non-verbal feedback. Once an orchestra captures the conductor's vision, it is obvious by the smile on his or her face and the power of the performance.

My Vision

To introduce you to the concept of vision, I want to share a bit of my own history and how having an eye on a clear goal, and then pursuing that goal with all my passion, allowed me to reach it. This vision or goal creation is important for company growth and movement, as well as personal growth.

My passion for playing music began when I was 12 years old and began playing the electric bass. I started playing the upright bass during my last year of High School. (This is the large wooden instrument in the back of the orchestra, not the ones you plugin).

Music changed my life and was, dare I use the term, instrumental in helping me grow and understand how a team works. The bass is the foundation of the orchestra. The tuba and some percussion instruments, such as the timpani (Kettle Drums) are also a form of bass. If you want to understand how important this is to music, turn on your radio. Now turn the treble up and the bass all the way down. How does it sound? Hollow right? Tinny?

I was the person who supported and was the foundation of, a large group of musicians. Who on your team or company plays that role? If there is not a foundation of a company or a strong leader, it is hard for the company to develop a vision and grow a company let alone create a strong project portfolio management culture.

By the time I was 17, I knew that I wanted to be a professional musician. I knew I needed more education and more practice. I had to really think about what it meant - what was my end game? I wanted to be a professional musician, and I wanted to do something that encompassed my faith, as well.

Every decision I made as far as education, whom I studied with, and where I was living, was based upon my vision. I had to establish what I wanted, and then each decision or crossroad was weighed against what I wanted. It made the process easier, and it brought me to my goals in a more direct fashion. The same can apply when you are working on the vision for your company, as it will permeate each project and your portfolio as a whole. Each project will have its own vision of what it looks like, and what it is to accomplish, but what works best is if the project vision is in harmony with the company's vision.

What I Learned Along the Way

As I grew into a professional musician, I began to learn lessons that helped me later in life when I shifted careers. This time, though, I had learned some important lessons from the conductors I had played under. I understood how they developed a vision and then executed it. I understood the process of not only developing of vision of a particular piece, but I understood how they developed a vision for the orchestra as an entity, and how they developed a theme for a particular season.

The season that an orchestra will perform for the next year is determined ahead of time. Sometimes the conductor may have a desire to perform certain pieces, and then develop a season around those pieces, or they may have a theme in mind, and then decide upon the pieces that would fit within that theme.

There are other factors such as soloists and different types of concerts (Holiday, Pops, or School Concerts) that are also factored in the decision. If a soloist is being considered for a particular piece they are prepared to perform, a conductor must decide whether they fit within the vision of the season. That vision of a season is PPM. It is the eagle's eye view of the company; its purpose, its vision, and what work will need to be done.

In the case of an orchestra, once a season is decided upon, then each concert is considered. What music will be performed? What will the instrumentation be? Who will be performing with the orchestra? This is still PPM as the conductor is setting up individual projects. Each concert may have multiple performances or music requirements. This can occur during the holiday season in which an orchestra can be called upon to play on multiple dates in different locations.

All of these decisions are made before a new season begins. This is important for a number of reasons. One, of course, is budget - does the orchestra have the budget to pay for the concerts? This would include venue costs, paying backstage personnel, paying musicians, paying the soloist, paying the conductor, and paying for the rights to perform the music. There can be many more expenses, and all of these must be considered at the PPM level. Many symphonies are nonprofit, and many rely on donations. Tickets sales alone would not cover the cost of a performance; there has to be patrons and contributors. All of this needs to be considered early in the PPM process because some serious decisions have to be made. It could mean cutting personnel, cutting out a rehearsal, or cutting a concert altogether. This PPM is essential before it ever gets to the project management stage - in this case, advertising, and rehearsals.

This can be a challenge because the conductor, often called the music director, has to ask themselves, "How do I create buy-in when we have to have cutbacks, but yet we still have to deliver a high performing organization to our patrons?"

Part of the PPM process is maintaining the integrity and brand of the organization. There cannot be the appearance of an orchestra in trouble or cutting corners because that could compromise a performance.

I know of an orchestra in North Carolina that was affected by the economy there. They had regular patrons in the NASCAR and furniture industry. When the furniture industry began sending work overseas, and NASCAR changed the way they were doing business, it had a direct effect upon the orchestra because contributions were swiftly and deeply affected. Something needed to be done, but they did not want to give the impression that the symphony's quality performances might not be up to par.

So they got creative.

The conductor changed the formation of the Symphony. He made it appear that there was the same number of musicians by switching where the string section sat. In this way, the symphony was able to cut the number of musicians without anyone really noticing. Instead of cutting a concert for the season, they cut the number of rehearsals for each concert by one. This made the musicians work harder in a shorter amount of time, but no one wanted to lose a concert.

In the following years, the economy picked up, and they were able to increase the size of the symphony once again, but they found they really did not need the extra rehearsal. The vision and image of the symphony was maintained through a tough spot through effective PPM execution.

Staying True to Your Vision

When you think Chick-Fil-A, what comes to mind? You might not be familiar with the franchise, but the title is pretty revealing - they sell chicken. In fact, their whole franchise is built upon, selling only chicken as the central protein in their food. It comes as a filet, fried, grilled, nugget or even chicken salad, but it is all about the chicken.

They have spent a lot of money on their campaign and slogan - "Eat More Chicken," or if the cows are writing it "Eat Mor Chickin," because of course, cows that paint on billboards cannot spell very well. They have capitalized on ads, billboards, commercials, toys, featuring cows protesting humans eating beef, and encouraging them to eat chicken instead.

So why have they opened a small chain of restaurants in Georgia called Truett's Grill, that offers hamburgers and even patty melts? It is named after the founder of Chick-Fil-A Truett Cathey. They still offer chicken selections in an old-style diner atmosphere where food is delivered to the table.

But why the change in their brand; the very central message of their company? Are they in trouble? Did they decide chicken was not enough to stay open?

The reality, and you would have to dig a little bit unless you lived in Georgia in the early 1960s, is that Chick-Fil-A actually started as the Dwarf Restaurant, which was a family service style restaurant. So really, this is drawing from the roots of the organization, not moving in a new direction. The problem is that when you read reviews about the Truett Grill, there is a lot of confusion of its connection to Chick-Fil-A.

In fact, Chick-Fil-A has three different types of restaurants - Dwarf House (named after the seven dwarves), Hapeville Dwarf House (the original restaurant), and Truett's Grill.

The company culture permeates all of these restaurants as family establishments, and none of them is open on Sunday. This practice is connected to Truett's strong Southern Baptist roots. The PPM has a unified culture in all of its holdings no matter whether they sell just chicken or not. Truett's vision has remained alive even as the company has grown.

As I have already mentioned, Truett Cathy had strong religious beliefs that shaped his company. The vision statement of his company is, "To glorify God by being a faithful steward of all that is entrusted to us. To have a positive influence on all who come in contact with Chick-Fil-A."

How does Chick-Fil-A enforce the rule that all franchises are closed on Sundays? All of the locations are corporate-owned and franchised. Cathy has stated, "I was not so committed to financial success that I was willing to abandon my principles and priorities. One of the most visible examples of this is our decision to close on Sunday. Our decision to close on Sunday was our way of honoring God and of directing our attention to things that mattered more than our business."

Creating a Shared Vision- Why is it Important?

In the article "To Lead, Create a Shared Vision," (Harvard Business Review), the authors, James Kouzes and Barry Posner, conducted a survey of tens of thousands of working people about what makes a good leader. The number one response was honesty, but the second might be a little surprising, "… the second-highest requirement of a leader is that he or she be forward-looking applied only to the leader role. Just 27% of respondents selected it as something they want in a colleague, whereas 72% wanted it in a leader. (Among respondents holding more-senior roles in organizations, the percentage was even greater, at 88 %). No other quality showed such a dramatic difference between leader and colleague."

Symphonies are not like rock bands. This may seem like an obvious statement, but I am referring to the vision of a symphony. Most of the symphonies that exist in the world today have been around for many years. How do they stay relevant, fresh, and therefore funded?

The conductor and the board have to consider these questions every year when they develop a symphony season. They have to anticipate what the donors and audiences desire. The conductor has to be listening to other orchestras, contemplating new music, and maybe working with composers to commission new pieces.

They have to look to the future of the symphony constantly, and both the audience and the members of the orchestra look to the conductor for this type of forward-looking leadership. For the members of the orchestra, it is exciting to play new pieces or challenge themselves to play older pieces better than they have before. The audience wants to be impressed by a program or a new soloist. These decisions are not made impulsively; they are often looked at years in advance.

The Suite

While I was attending graduate school, I was invited to play in the pit orchestra of the Nutcracker Suite for the Cincinnati Ballet. It was a unique experience I will always remember because while I played, I could watch the ballet. It was one I had heard and seen before on television, and even though it was something I knew, the experience of seeing it live, and seeing their interpretation of the music was mesmerizing.

In Winston-Salem, North Carolina there exists an arts school, the University of North Carolina School of the Arts, where Tchaikovsky's The Nutcracker Suite has been performed every year since 1965. It involves all of the departments of the school in the yearly production - music (full symphony), dance, design and production, and drama department.

Each year there is a new set of students performing a couple dozen performances during the month of December. It is the same music and the same choreography every year. Costumes are modified and reused, and the lighting plot is the same every year. So what keeps it fresh? How does the director keep the audiences coming back a year to year?

Part of the answer, of course, is that parents come to see their kids perform and that it is part of a holiday tradition. Part of the answer is that it is a new cast, and so the performance is all new to them.

These performances are not free, and in fact, they raise money for their scholarship and for the upkeep of the auditorium. In 2014, the show raised $500,000, which broke the previous record amount in 2013 of $476,661. There had to be some forward-looking going on.

In 2009, the show's director, Ethan Stiefel, decided to do something new and reimagined the choreography for parts of the show. It was such a success that in 2015 he is returning to update some of the choreography in other parts of the show.

There had to be buy-in from the 80 students performing in the show. Many of them play more than one role. Creating new choreography changed the way the show was produced. For over forty years, the same dance steps were performed, and so the teaching of those steps became standard and efficient. Now everything had to be taught in a new way.

This meant many hours of practice. I mean a lot. You may work 40 hours a week or about 160 hours a month. You go home at the end of the day and relax until you have to do your 8-9 hours the next day. You also get off on the weekends and holidays. These students had to go to school all day; many of them were middle school and high school students, and so they spend a good portion of their day in classes, then dance classes and homework. Each of those students spent individually over 250 hours to learn their parts in the newly imagined ballet in the span of about three weeks.

They were not only dedicated to their craft, but they were dedicated to the vision of the director. They wanted to put in the hours needed to make an excellent show. Without a strong leader and dedication to working with that leader for many hours late into the night, the production would not be topping over a half a million dollars in sales every year. The director knew that parents and tradition were not enough; he needed to push the production in new directions, and the audiences and students loved it.

How do you create a Shared Vision?

Here are some questions to begin to consider when working on your company Vision:
- Why are we doing this?
- What is your company's mission?
- What is important to us about this?
- What will the results look like?
- What outcomes do we seek?
- Is this consistent with your beliefs and values?

Sometimes it is tough to know where to begin, so here are some simple steps to get started.

Step 1: What are you working on?

Be clear about the purpose of your vision. Is it for the entire company, or is it for a particular project? The clearer you are at this step, the easier it will be later in the process.

Step 2: Choose parameters

How far is the vision looking into the future? Is this short term or long term. Many organizations look anywhere from two to ten years into the future, but the average is about five.

Step 3: List wins

Make a list of positives- achievements, successes, and skills you and your colleagues have acquired that could contribute to the success of your vision. The point is to infuse your vision with a positive momentum.

Step 4: Write it down

Once you begin to form the vision, be sure to write it down. It should be in the form of something that is currently occurring, not something that might happen in the future. Be passionate and connected as you create the vision.

Step 5: Work on the draft

Once you have a working draft of your vision, go back and refine, and massage it into something better. Be sure that it sounds inspiring and that you are excited when you read it. Use measurable outcomes that are concise rather than vague ones.

Step 6: Rework it again

Take some time between Step 5 and 6. Allow it to sink in and digest what you have done. Then take it again, and determine if it has the same punch. Rework it half a dozen more times until you are sure it is absolutely spot on. It should be tight and focused while being moving and inspiring.

Step 7: Solicit feedback

Once you have completed the last step, it is time to allow others to read it and solicit their input. You should decide upon the best people to read it, and the ones that will give you the most helpful feedback. Some people will talk about the action steps, and this will be relevant later, so just listen and take notes. Be sure to stay on task at this point about the outcome- the vision, and not necessarily how you will get there.

Step 8: Share it

Once you are sure you are happy with the outcome, it is time to share the vision with everyone. You will have many people asking questions; many of them about how to implement the vision. Be sure to be clear that this is the "what," and the next step will be the "how."

The Seven Steps

You have enjoyed just the first step in"7 STEPS TO CREATING HIGH-PERFORMING TEAMS!" Below are summations all of the seven principles to give you the ability to unpack PPM strategies that will transform and grow your company.

Vision: A great culture starts with a vision or mission statement. As my friend Dr. Willie Jolley says, "Without a vision, people perish, but with a vision people flourish."

Values: A company's values are the core of its culture. While a vision articulates a company's purpose, values offer a set of guidelines on the behaviors and mindsets needed to achieve that vision.

Buy-In: No company can build a coherent culture without people who either share its core values or possess the willingness and ability to embrace those values. That's why the greatest firms in the world also have some of the most stringent recruiting policies.

Best Practices: Values are of little importance unless they are enshrined in a company's practices. If an organization professes, "people are our greatest asset," it should also be ready to invest in people in visible ways.

Stories: All organizations have a unique history - a unique story. The ability to unearth that history and craft it into a narrative is a core element of culture creation.

Environment: Consider Pixar; they have a huge open atrium – they have developed an environment where the firm members are able to connect throughout the day and interact in informal, unplanned ways. Mayor Michael Bloomberg has designed his workspace into a "bullpen" where he and his staff sit, rather than in separate offices that are stuffy and soundproof. Moreover, consider tech firms that cluster in Silicon Valley or financial firms selecting to cluster in London and New York. There are obviously numerous answers to each of these questions, but one clear answer is that place shapes culture.

Execution: People Respect What You Inspect. Team members make a commitment to the team, not to the leader, and they hold each other accountable.

Questions to Consider

1. What is your dream or vision for the future of your organization?
2. How will you align your vision with your mission, goals, and objectives, key strategies, tactics, and allocation of resources?
3. What demands will your future strategy make on the quality and quantity of people that you need?
4. As you think about the future of your business or organization, what are you most excited about?
5. What are you most worried about?

Strategies for Application

1. Create your mission statement. What is your organization's compelling idea? What makes your organization stand out from its competition? Whom do you want to become and what impact do you want your organization to have in the market and on your community?
2. Next, create your vision statement. What will you and your stakeholder's value the most for your organization, agency, department, or family? Combine your mission statement and your values together to create a compelling vision statement.

Additional Resources

- Case Study of Bad Culture
  http://www.chicagomag.com/Chicago-Magazine/September-2014/What-Happened-to-Motorola/

- 5 Myths of Great Workplaces
  https://hbr.org/2015/03/5-myths-of-great-workplaces

CHAPTER 3

VALUES

V alues must be embraced, and not just hung on a plaque. We must live them; they can't be empty hollow words. They have to have an intrinsic value from the bottom to the top of an organization. These values will permeate every project, and more importantly, every employee.

> *"Your beliefs become your thoughts. Your thoughts become your words. Your words become your actions. Your actions become your habits. Your habits become your values. Your values become your destiny." — Mahatma Gandhi*

One of the toughest times in the career of a musician is when they are hired to be a part of a large ensemble. There is, of course, the expectation that they can play their part with expert precision. For most professionals, this is not a problem. By the time they reach the level of professional musician, they have spent thousands of hours practicing.

What is tougher is for that musician to acclimate themselves to the culture. What values does the symphony follow? What are the expectations? They can be as simple as arriving 15 minutes early, and be warmed up and ready well before the conductor ever takes the podium to begin a rehearsal.

It could be that they attend a Thursday night chamber music session at one of the musician's homes. This is not a written rule, but it is definitely an unwritten expectation. The value is that the musicians spend time outside the hall to bond, share, and create. What happens if they blow off that Thursday night get together?

According to Patrick Lencioni, there are four different kinds of values within an organization, which I will discuss below. The value types are:

- Core Values
- Aspirational Values
- Permission to Play Values
- Accidental Values

Core Values are those that are immovable. These are the foundational values that dictate and move a company's values. These cannot be violated or compromised. In a symphony, a universal value is that you come prepared for rehearsal. There is no excuse for missing music, forgetting your bow, or not practicing a piece before rehearsal. These are non-negotiables. Sure, things can happen, but it is still not excusable long term. The reason these values are strong, both in a symphony and in business, is that they affect everyone. If a musician is not prepared, it can throw off an entire rehearsal.

If I were to forget my bass bow, I would not only get head shakes or a possible dressing down by the conductor, but everyone in my section would give me the same cold indifference. At the level of professional musician, the value is that you are prepared - period.

Core values can affect the brand of a company- which is why it cannot be compromised. Consider Disney World; what is their main theme, their value to their customers?

It's the happiest place on Earth. Right?

If someone is frowning, or in a bad mood and displays this, how does that affect the happiest place on Earth? If you have ever been to Disney World, especially with small children, you will know, it is in fact NOT the happiest place on Earth. Why? Because it's often hot, the kids are tired, and the lines are long, long, around another bend long.

How does Disney then maintain the feeling of happy? First, they overstate and then outperform. If you are in a line, and the sign says 45 minutes to the ride, you may feel exasperated. The kids are hungry, your feet hurt, and you're tired. 20 minutes later, you are on Dumbo's back flying high in the sky, and your kids are squealing with joy. You are happy. Why? Because you thought you had to wait 45 minutes, but you only waited for 20. They overstated and over performed to get you on that ride. It is totally on purpose because their value permeates everything they do.

A colleague of mine, John, went to Disney World recently and came back with a story. His three-year-old son was not feeling good. It was too hot the day they went, everyone was tired from their vacation, and little Max was crying loudly in a backroom of one of the onsite restaurants. It was so loud that a group of staff members at the restaurant came to see little Max and here is what they said, "Our boss, Mickey told us we needed to see you. He told us that you were having a tough time and that we needed to make you smile because that is what Mickey is all about - smiles. So he told us to bring you something special. I have to report back to Mickey that you smiled."

They handed Max a gift they were selling in the shop for about $20.00. But it was not the monetary issue; it was the attention they gave to that little boy. He smiled, laughed and talked to the staff members about his day and what the other rides he wanted to see. He left with a smile.

No one ordered the staff to do that; it was just a core value. Every child is happy. Every child is smiling if it is in their power to create. They created that smile and maintained for that family that it was the happiest place on Earth.

There are some values that a company aspires to, but that they lack. They are going after these values, and it may take work to achieve them. In an orchestra, starting their concert right at 8:05 may be an aspirational value. They want everyone to be seated, everyone warmed up and ready to play, and the audience quiet and attentive. Everyone in the orchestra and the audience may be aware of this aspirational value of being on time, and there may be a dimming of the lights at 8:03 PM to remind everyone, but even with the best efforts the concert may be consistently delayed.

Aspirational values are not the same as core values. When these are confused, and crossover occurs, there may be confusion. If the orchestra is all classically trained musicians, but the conductor insists on always choosing pops and jazz pieces, there can be confusion, especially if the orchestra is not known to be a Pops orchestra, like the Boston Pops.

As you may have surmised, vision and values are very closely related. Vision drives and develops values.

Permission to play values are standards within a company that are not core but are values of high value within an organization. Suppose a symphony boasted that they had a drug free workplace. They did not abide by musicians who did illegal and illicit drugs. This is a permission to play value unless the symphony had a strict drug use policy and drug tested the musicians on a rotating and random basis as a condition of their employment. If they had such strict policies, then you could say that was a core value, but if you generally frowned upon the use of drugs, but had no direct policies to address it, then it becomes a permission to play value. A conductor might say, "We would love for you to play for our orchestra, but if you come in high, then you may be asked to go home and sober up before the next rehearsal."

Accidental values occur more organically. They are not cultivated by leadership, and they seem to have a mind of their own, and they develop over time. Practical jokes can be an example. Suppose whenever the boss is out of the office for a few days, the group does something outrageous and funny, like rearranging the bosses' office, wrapping everything in plastic wrap, or messing with their computer. Now, this may encourage community spirit, and it may make all the workers feel like they are a part of something fun and cool. The boss, of course, would not be sanctioning it, and so they have a choice.

If it is all in play and things do not get out of hand, and it does not interfere with a core value of making production on time, then they may allow this accidental value to continue, as new employees may be indoctrinated and feel like they are a part of something special.

However, if the accidental value does not align or interferes with a core value, then a leader may need to address it and redirect it.

As part of the last concert of the year in college, someone would slip some funny picture somewhere random in the conductor's score. Everyone in the orchestra knew what was going on, and really so did the conductor. It was a shared joke that brought the orchestra together with the conductor. The value is having fun and communicating how much both the leader and the team appreciate one another. When a freshman comes in, they hear the stories and are excited to be a part of the harmless prank.

> *"A mission statement is not something you write overnight... But fundamentally, your mission statement becomes your constitution, the solid expression of your vision and values. It becomes the criterion by which you measure everything else in your life."*
>
> *Stephen Covey*

A company's values are the core of its culture. While a vision articulates a company's purpose, values offer a set of guidelines on the behaviors and mindsets needed to achieve that vision. McKinsey & Company, for example, has a clearly articulated set of values that are prominently communicated to all employees and involve the way that firm vows to serve clients, treat colleagues, and uphold professional standards.

McKinsey's Values

- Adhere to the highest professional standards
- Put client interests ahead of the firm.
- Observe high ethical standards.
- Preserve client confidences.
- Maintain an independent perspective.
- Manage client and firm resources cost-effectively.
- Improve our clients' performance significantly.
- Follow the top-management approach.
- Use our global network to deliver the best of the firm to all clients.
- Bring innovations in management practice to clients.
- Build client capabilities to sustain improvement.
- Build enduring relationships based on trust.
- Create an unrivaled environment for exceptional people
- Be nonhierarchical and inclusive.
- Sustain a caring meritocracy.
- Develop one another through apprenticeship and mentoring.
- Uphold the obligation to dissent.
- Govern ourselves as a "One Firm" partnership.

http://www.mckinsey.com.ar/our_work_belive.asp

John Willard Marriott was a connector of people and always treated his employees as the most important part of his business life. An effective leader knows how to challenge others to work toward organizational goals. The most important role a leader can possess is to believe in one common goal and to work hard for a unified purpose. It is important to maintain composure during tough times because subordinates will turn to organizational leaders during trying times.

His credo was, "Take care of your employees, and they'll take care of your customers." Bill Marriott, his son, expounded on this concept when he delivered a speech in 2000 to the Economic Club of Detroit. The name of the talk was "Our Competitive Strength: Human Capital."

In his speech, he shared five guiding principles related to their credo:

1.   **Get it right the first time.** He stated that they would rather hire the right person, who already personified the values of the spirit to serve, and train them to work in a hotel, rather than training someone with a lot of hospitality business experience and try to instill in them the value of treating each guest with dignity and the respect they deserved. The value and buy-in are more important. Bill said that it is hard to teach someone to smile when they don't do it naturally. They can be trained the technical skills much easier.

2.   **Money is a big thing, but it's not the only thing.** The philosophy is what is good for the customers is also good for the employees. This is true when it comes to money - and Marriott offers competitive wages, but that is not the only thing they focus on - they are committed to providing a great workplace, which includes intangible things like work-life balance, quality leadership, the opportunity for advancement, a healthy and safe work environment, and training. Marriot has found that these factors are more important for retention than money alone.

3.   **A caring workplace is a bottom-line issue.** Often when a guest arrives at a hotel, all they want is a hot shower and bed because they are travel weary. Marriot is committed to giving it's associate's genuine care, dependability, and a sense of community. This means that the associates may feel good about where they work- they need to feel safe, secure and welcome just as the guests are. Bill's father, in the early days, would sit on the couch in the lobby of one of his first hotels and help his associates talk through some of their personal issues and challenges. As the chain grew, of course, Marriott could no longer be there for every associate, but he was committed to the same value that the workplace should be safe, secure and welcoming. He transferred the responsibility to the managers of the hotels, by making them responsible for associate satisfaction and turnover rates. Managers are responsible for conducting 15-minute interviews for each department daily. In these meetings, the associates can raise personal concerns and their birthdays and other special dates are acknowledged and celebrated.

4.   **Promote from within.** One of the driving ideas at Marriott is, "Culture is the life-thread and glue that links our past, present, and future." They are dedicated to the value of promoting within their ranks rather than looking for talent from outside the corporation. They groom and provide support and encouragement in order to help pass on the soul of the business to others. Over 50 percent of Marriott managers have been promoted in this manner.

5.   **Build your brand for your Associates.** Guests have unlimited choices when it comes to the hotel they stay at. More importantly, Marriot works hard at branding their chain to create customer loyalty. They have incorporated this same idea for their employees and work equally as hard at branding the company for their employees to want to work for them because it is a "great place" to work. They work hard at creating a brand that their employees become loyal to and talk about, not only to their guests but to other potential employees.

Stay True to Your Values

It is not only important for a company to have strong values, but they also must be true to those values. If they say they value something, they must also put that value into action.

There was a study conducted at the Einaudi Institute for Economics and Finance and Paola Sapienza of Northwestern University by Luigi Zingales and Luigi Guiso that studied two questions:
- How corporate culture affects companies?
- How all kinds of financial decisions at those companies affect the ongoing culture?

They used a dataset created by the Great Place to Work (GPTW) Institute, which conducts extensive surveys of employees at more than 1,000 US firms. The data sets surrounded two important statements:
- Management's actions match its words.
- Management is honest and ethical in its business practices.

In addition, they also gathered information from Standard and Poor's 500 companies in order to get a peek at how companies presented their corporate cultures to the world. They found that at least 85% of the companies they researched had at least one page dedicated to what they describe as a corporate culture as defined by the principles and values that should inform the behavior of everyone who works for their company. The values, in the order listed by 80% of the companies, were:

- Innovation
- Integrity
- Respect
- Teamwork.

What they found interesting is that the values listed had little to do with the profitability of the company or performance. Further, a company that has a culture based on integrity, at least as perceived by the employees of that company, added to the value of that company. Therefore, when the top management upholds the values, it supports the value in the eyes of the employees, and it becomes part of the culture of the company; it becomes the norm. Conversely, a breach in the trust of management not upholding those values can lead to a culture collapse, which can have widespread implications.

It is true that the decision to uphold the values and having integrity can have short-term implications because some can sacrifice customer satisfaction, but this is the difference between short-term loss and long-term value. Integrity is what keeps the company together. Strong corporate culture leads to strong performance.

Questions to Consider

1. What values within you do you feel are most representative of the company culture you would like to see surrounding you?
2. How would you like your company to be managed?
3. Do you conceive of particular organizational approaches that would create your ideal company?
4. Do you have a specific management style you would like to follow?
5. Do you envision particular behaviors, attitudes, and dress for your team?
6. Do you envision distinctive operations (superior efficiency, quality control, innovative methods, or technology)?

Strategies for Application

1. Brainstorm ideas that your organization can leverage to build a database of guiding principles or values.
2. Develop an Affinity Diagram to capture your organization's guiding principle themes. An Affinity Diagram is a tool for organizing ideas in a very efficient manner.
3. Prioritize the guiding principle themes until you have your core values identified.
4. Document your organization's values into 4 categories and develop a plan to address any accidental values you do not desire to permeate in your environment.
   a. Core Values
   b. Aspirational Values
   c. Permission to Play Values
   d. Accidental Values

Additional Resources

- 10 Steps For Developing Your Company's Core Values
  http://deliveringhappiness.com/services/10-steps-for-developing-core-values/
- A Values-Based Path to Collaboration
  https://www.valuescentre.com/sites/default/files/case-studies/YN-HHS_Case_Study.pdf
- WHAT IS AN AFFINITY DIAGRAM? https://www.spcforexcel.com/knowledge/process-improvement/affinity-diagrams
- Quote by Gandhi: Your beliefs become your thoughts, Your., http://www.goodreads.com/quotes/50584-your-beliefs-become-your-thoughts-your-tho (accessed June 24, 2016).
- Six Components of a Great Corporate Culture, https://hbr.org/2013/05/six-components-of-culture/ (accessed June 24, 2016).
- Strong corporate culture leads to strong performance, http://review.chicagobooth.edu/economics/2014/article/strong-corporate-culture-l (accessed June 24, 2016).

- McKinsey & Company - Buenos Aires Office, http://www.mckinsey.com.ar/our_work_belive.asp (accessed June 24, 2016).
- HBR Blog Network - Lauren E. Case, http://laurencase.weebly.com/uploads/2/3/4/0/23401906/six_components_of_a_great_ (accessed June 24, 2016).

CHAPTER 4

BUY-IN

I t is not enough to just have a vision for a company if you don't have buy-in from the people within your company. It is like building a bridge to nowhere. You have your vision statement on every signature line on emails, in bright letters painted in the lobby of your company, or even a song written about it, and without buy-in, the dedication and action toward that vision, it is nothing more than pretty words.

In a symphony, buy-in is huge. It occurs on a few different levels. First is the buy-in by the board of the symphony. If they do not believe in what the symphony is about and believe in what the symphony represents to a community, then they will not put resources and time towards supporting the vision.

A friend recently told me of a story about approaching his symphony board about increasing the pay for musicians. My friend was a personnel manager and was attempting to recruit the best musicians he could to make the symphony a shining jewel in the community. The community where the symphony resides was hard hit by the recession and many businesses left to open up factories overseas. The symphony represented a culture that was desperately needed.

The conductor had increased the number of in-school concerts, and other outdoor events to bring the community together. At the same time, he wanted to increase the reputation of the symphony as the best in their state and region. He was having more commissioned pieces performed and the recordings submitted to international music competitions.

All of this meant the symphony required the best musicians, but to attract them, the personnel manager had to offer competitive rates of pay. The symphony had not had any salary increases in some years, even though endowments and grants had increased.

It was time for my friend to make a case to the board, which was that in order to achieve the vision of the orchestra, they needed to approve the price increase proposed. The board was not on board.

One of the board members was a medical doctor, and after listening to the presentation, and looking at the proposal said, "Why do they need more money. I mean, after all, this is just a hobby right?"

Even though there was a clear vision, there was no buy-in to what needed to occur in order to support and articulate that vision. The proposal was turned down, and so the orchestra struggled to get the best musicians to audition.

> *"People buy into the leader before they buy into the vision."*
>
> *John C. Maxwell*

Another layer of buy-in of an orchestra is buy-in of the musicians and audience to the conductor's vision as demonstrated in his programming. If the conductor is married to the idea that the orchestra is a contemporary music group, he must convince the musicians of the programming. He must equally convince the audience, to keep their attention, and to ensure their attendance. If there is not buy-in, the audience may complain that they are not hearing the standards they are used to hearing- Bach, Beethoven, and Mozart. They may, over time, begin to appreciate the vision of the conductor, but if they if they feel the vision is forced, they will not have buy-in.

If the musicians are not playing the music, they are expected to be playing; they may look for other venues and orchestras. This is not uncommon in corporations. If a new vision is rolled out within an organization without buy-in-two things are likely to happen. Resistance and turn over. Some of this is normal and healthy for an organization, but too much, and morale of those that remain could be negatively affected.

Finally, the orchestra must have the buy-in of the conductor's vision of a piece. Much resistance can occur if a conductor decides to perform a piece of music significantly different from the way it is normally played. Orchestra's, for the most part, are authoritarian in their structure, the conductor is always right, but be that as it may, they must have buy-in from the players. If they do not explain why they have a particularly new way of interpreting a piece, the musicians could become resistant to playing it the new way.

This can cause irritation and wasted rehearsal time, and it could sink a performance. Alternatively, the audience may also be disappointed that in Beethoven's Fifth Symphony—Da Da Da DAAAAAA, the opening is more. Da......
Da.......Da..... DAA. The conductor's vision may be clear to them, but without explanation and context, they will lose the necessary buy-in from musicians and audience.

When people walk into a symphony concert, they are handed a program. In it, a conductor can write about their vision and reasons they approached a particular piece in a certain way, and this can greatly create buy-in and temper expectations.

Buy-In Starts with the Right People

"No company can build a coherent culture without people who either share its core values or possess the willingness and ability to embrace those values. That's why the greatest firms in the world also have some of the most stringent recruiting policies."
(https://hbr.org/2013/05/six-components-of-culture)

It starts by hiring the right people that share a company's vision from the beginning because they will have greater buy-in. Remember, in my story about Marriott that he was committed to hiring people that were committed to his vision, even if they did not have a lot of hospitality industry experience. He knew that it was more valuable for them to have buy-in because skills can be taught.

"If you want to build a ship, don't drum up people together to collect wood and don't assign them tasks and work, but rather teach them to long for the endless immensity of the sea." Antoine de Saint-Exupery

Why is Buy-In Essential?

The answer is directly tied to employee engagement, which we have already established is essential for retention. Here are some statistics from Gallup, the Incentive Federation, the Incentive Research Foundation, Maritz, and World at Work. (http://www.bhengagement.com/23-employee-motivation-statistics-to-silence-na...)

- 90% of business leaders believe that an engagement strategy could positively impact their business, yet only 25% of them actually have a strategy in place.
- 39% of employees feel underappreciated at work, with 77% reporting that they would work harder if they felt better recognized.
- According to a recent CareerBuilder/USA Today survey, 56% of HR managers are worried that their top talent will leave for another job within the year.
- 75% of people who willingly leave their jobs don't quit their jobs; they quit their bosses.
- A 5% increase in employee retention can generate a 25% to 85% increase in profitability.
- 41% of customers are loyal to a brand or company because they consistently notice a positive employee attitude, while 68% of customers defect from a brand or company because of negative employee attitude.
- Only 40% of employees are well informed of their company's goals, strategy, and tactics.

"Engaged organizations grew profits as much as three times faster than their competitors. They report that highly engaged organizations have the potential to reduce staff turnover by 87% and improve performance by 20%." (Source: Corporate Leadership Council)

People have to feel the Problem

It is great if you can have control of people buying into the company's vision by hiring the right people, but what can you do about the people that are already in an organization? In John Kotter's piece for the HBR (https://hbr.org/2011/02/before-you-can-get-buy-in-peop.html), he states that people have to feel the pain of the problem first before they can buy into the vision, which is the solution. You have to make it real for those you are trying to get to buy-in.

Back to my story about the personnel manager of the symphony, he had a real issue on his hands. He knew what the vision of the conductor was, which was to have the best of the best playing in the orchestra, but the board, made up of non-musicians could not fully grasp the problem. So my friend created and executed a plan to get the board to truly understand the issue and the vision.

My friend invited musicians to perform some excerpts from the season's lineup of concerts. He chose a musician from each section. After they had played, each musician talked about their education, how many years they played, what their instruments cost, and what their upkeep was. He had them describe their struggles as a musician financially, as all of them were professional musicians that were often forced to get second and third jobs to survive.

After a couple of board meetings, and hearing from the musicians, the board unanimously voted to increase the pay scale over the next five years to get the orchestra at least to the point of being competitive with other orchestras their size and in their market.

Change is Tough

During private lessons to learn an instrument, a teacher will give you a passage to practice. You are expected to then perform the piece or excerpt at the next lesson. One of the worst things that can happen is if you are playing a rhythm or playing a wrong note consistently because you end up practicing it, you have then embedded the wrong sequence. It is easier to learn something the right way, then to relearn something and to have to change it because you learned it the wrong way.

Change happens in companies much the same way. Employees can become used to thinking a certain way about their job and how they perform it. When you introduce a new change, such as a vision, it can create issues. People can become frustrated or even resistant to change. This can cause issues with buy-in. Some companies hire special coaches or even teams to come to help in the process of change. They can anticipate where the problems will arise, and how many employees they may lose, but most importantly they can provide them with strategies to make the change and the adoption of new ideas (vision) to go as smoothly and as quickly as possible.

Preparing for Change

Below is a strategy to roll out change, specifically eliciting buy-in for a company's vision. Here are some important areas to consider and work on before trying to roll out a new direction and vision for your employees.

1. **What is the organizational environment?** The structure of your organization can have an impact on how change occurs and how information is disseminated. Does your company have a partnership structure, or do people work within silos? Is the culture based on trust? Is there an open dialog? Are people fearful of being fired for speaking up? The best possible structure is based on trust, safety, and partnerships. You may have to make some adjustments in this area, or people may not be open to other changes that they feel may put them at risk. Try to remove fear from your culture and create a more open dialog that is supported by management.

2. **Be sure that your vision has credibility.** In the last chapter, we talked about how to create a solid vision, but will it work? Provide data and examples of where your vision has worked either within your company or other companies. Build their confidence before they are required to implement the changes. This ensures buy-in from the beginning. Remember that is not what you believe will work; it is what others believe that creates buy-in.

3. **Start from the top.** The more buy-in you have from C-level and managers, the better chance you have of others buying into your vision. There is strength and momentum in numbers. The more people that are on board, the greater strength you will have to convince others to adopt change. Target key people that have the credibility and respect in your company to speak about the benefits of your vision and how it will change the company in a positive way. Don't try to force changes, as this will cause resistance; rather pave a smooth path and invite people to participate in the change.

4. **There is the WIII FM.** It is the official radio channel in most companies, and it is What Is In It For Me. People will have their own agendas and their own visions, and so you must try to align everyone to one vision. You have to be clear about what the benefits are in following and implementing your vision. Listen to what they have to say, and what their concerns are, but be prepared to

answer those questions and turn it back into a benefit for everyone. Use the word "we" when referring to the vision. Include everyone, and everyone will feel included. This turns off the WIII FM because people will think about what is better for everyone rather than just themselves.

5. **Be sure that everyone knows the ROI on accepting and implementing change.** People respond to money talk, and if you can demonstrate how following a vision will translate into dollars and cents, people will become more attentive and more likely to buy-in if they feel that it can translate into more benefits and better pay. Connect the dots for them, but do not oversell or overpromise, rather help them to see and commit to the vision of what "could" or "might" be if everyone worked together.

Strategic Plan for Change

Below I have laid out a strategy for the actual rollout of a vision for the company. You can use these same steps for rolling out any major change for a company to adopt.

1. Go back to Chapter 2 and be clear about your vision. Make sure it is refined, and the language is clear.

2. Be sure everyone has what he or she needs to implement the change. Don't assume everyone is prepared, check-in with managers and be sure everyone is prepared has what they need.

3. Check-in with managers and employees often to ensure people know what is happening, the expectations, and to receive feedback about progress. You can send out emails, or newsletters, or set up periodic meetings. Keep the channels of communication open; don't assume anything.

4. Be sure everyone is involved. When creating a plan for your company, involve every person and department. Don't leave anyone out. This makes everyone feel that they are valued, and it reduces negative feelings about their importance. Give everyone opportunities to contribute and provide feedback about ways things can improve even further. Invite them to create and implement their own projects within their teams.

5. Provide positive feedback often. People want to know they are doing a good job. Tell people thank you in a way that makes them feel valued and appreciated. It could be a private message, a card, or a mention in a meeting. If you

have to give negative feedback, do it quickly, provide solutions, and the opportunity for others to correct their mistakes.

6.   Spend time knowing your employees. Make it seem like you are one of them, rather than sitting on high. Relate to them, and they will be more honest and feel much more appreciated. Create trust and respect.

7.   Make the change fun. Be creative. Have a smile on your face and talk in positive tones. Have fun competitions within the organization. The process does not have to be labor-intensive and painful.

8.   Review your vision and your process of implementation at regular intervals. As I mentioned earlier, a vision is a living and breathing thing. It will change and need to be changed over time as trends change in your industry, when there are new employees, or even if you change what it is you are producing. You have to be flexible and prepared to make adjustments. It is critical that you have buy-in when these changes occur, and that you are getting as much feedback as possible to make the best decisions.

Questions to Consider

1. Here's a list of questions to generate Buy-In from your team.
2. How do you feel our collaboration is going?
3. What do you feel is working, not working, and what should we keep doing?
4. Are we communicating consistently and sufficiently enough for you to feel plugged in and aware of the organization's strategic direction and change efforts?
5. Do you feel we are working on the most central and critical issues to move our organization forward based on our current vision, mission, goals, and objectives?

Strategies for Application

*   Develop a RACI chart of your key process. A RACI chart also called a RAM chart, is used to identify roles and responsibility for a team during an organizational change process. RACI stands for Responsible, Accountable, Consulted and Informed. https://en.wikipedia.org/wiki/Responsibility_assignment_matrix

- Have your team take the **PERMA Model** assessment developed by Dr. Martin E. P. Seligman. By focusing on these items, your team can identify their true individual purposes and learn to align themselves with your organization's culture and overall direction. Here's the PERMA Model:

  - o Positive - is inheritable (Hunt the Good Stuff)
  - o Engagement (Optimism and Optimal Performance)
  - o Relationships (ACR)
  - o Meaning and Purpose (Fun vs. Altruism)
  - o Achievement (GRIT)
  - o Invisible Hand
- www.AuthenticHappiness.org

Additional Resources

- Helping employees embrace change
  http://www.mckinsey.com/business-functions/organization/our-in-sights/helping-employees-embrace-change
- How To Get Employee Buy-in To Build Exceptional Culture
  http://www.fastcompany.com/3001573/how-get-employee-buy-build-ex-ceptional-culture
- John C. Maxwell quotes - ThinkExist.com, http://thinkex-ist.com/quotation/people_buy_into_the_leader_be-fore_they_buy_into/ (accessed June 24, 2016).
- Six Components of a Great Corporate Culture, https://hbr.org/2013/05/six-components-of-culture/ (accessed June 24, 2016).
- Radical Positivity | Building People To Build People, http://www.itsradicalpositivity.com/ (accessed June 24, 2016).
- Social Knows: Employee Engagement Statistics (August 2011 .., http://www.thesocialworkplace.com/2011/08/social-knows-em-ployee-engagement-stati (accessed June 24, 2016).

CHAPTER 5

STORIES

"Storytelling is the most powerful way to put ideas into the world today." --Robert McKee

S tories can be very powerful in an organization. They can bridge the gap between the past, present, and future. They can create a dialog between generations. They inspire and teach and provide a framework for an organization.

Every organization has a story, as does everyone within that organization. When you join an organization, you become part of that story. You will hear about the organization's history, the key players that made that organization great, and you then become part of that legacy. Within symphonies, there can be turnover. Musicians move on to different organizations; some retire, some may go on tour with a smaller group. There is usually a pool of replacements that can be called on in a pinch, and most symphonies hold auditions for open slots.

When you sit down for the first time and play, unless you are the first chair within a section, you have a person sitting on both sides of you. The bass section is the exception to the sharing of the stand situation, but in larger symphonies, there can be some sharing. This means two people are looking at the same music on one music stand. There may be more than one part on the music, and musicians may be playing two different parts in a particular piece.

Becoming a new member, there are a few questions you have to get out of the way, such as which one of you is going to mark the music, and which one is turning pages. However, the conversation will inevitably turn to learning the new musician's story. The other players want to know where the person came from, where they went to school, and what other ensembles they played with.

There are a few reasons this occurs, and don't get me wrong; everyone expects this. It is not like an inquisition.

First, the other players are trying to determine how good the player is. They want to know that they truly earned their place in the symphony. For some, it is about sizing up the competition, but for most, they are deciding whether this person is an asset to the section, or will be a liability and need help.

The second reason is that sections of an orchestra are like smaller family units at a family reunion. They want to find some common ground with the person sitting next to them.

"Oh, when did you go to the Manhattan School of Music? I went there in 1980. Did you have to take music theory from Dr. Klein? Oh, man was he hard. There was, this time, he…"

Then other people will begin sharing their personal stories. They find that common ground and then use it to form a bond with the new person, and the new person uses it to become one of the family of players.

Over time the players, the ones that are the old-timers, will begin to share their stories about the symphony and the music and the stories about performing the music. They will compare conductors and soloists and venues. This provides context to the other players. They learn from the stories about what to expect, what has worked in the past, and what was a disaster. The veterans often "adopt" new players to show the ropes - which usually includes a list of what not to do at rehearsal.

"Always be on time. The conductor once locked the doors one minute after the rehearsal started and prevented the late players from coming in. They were docked on their pay. I can tell you; they were never late again."

"Bring a pencil. The maestro expects you to write what he says down because if not, he will call you out on it. One time the principal oboe player missed an entrance. The conductor explained how he was going to cue the oboe player, and then followed it up with, 'Why aren't you writing this down? Do you have a photographic memory or something? I expect you to use that pencil on your stand and write down what I am saying because I will not repeat myself. You will find yourself lost and looking for a new place to honk your oboe.'"

(NOTE- Conductors are not always known for their tact. They are essentially dictators, and some play the part very well.)

If you were that oboe player that was schooled in front of the orchestra, you would now have a new story to pass on to someone else. Maybe for a laugh, or as a warning, but either way, the story is important.

"The stories we tell literally make the world. If you want to change the world, you need to change your story. This truth applies both to individuals and institutions." --*Michael Margolis*

In the previous chapters, I talked about vision, values, and buy-in. The stories are what carries and send the vision across the organization and beyond. Stories contain the values of the organization and the people within it, and stories are essential for buy-in. Stories can draw people in, or repel them. As a leader, it is important to listen to the stories around you, and more importantly to know when and what stories to share with others.

"There's always room for a story that can transport people to another place." --*J.K. Rowling*

My Father's Tale

At my father's funeral, his brother-in-law Rev. Reed, who leads a church in Baltimore, preached his eulogy. After listening to the sharing from family and friends, dad's golfing buddies, and others, Rev. Reed stated that someone should write a book about an ordinary hard-working man who raised an extraordinary family. My uncle, Samuel Jackson, called my father "one of the hardest working men I've ever known." He was amazed at the level of strength my dad had and could not understand how someone could work so hard and provide so much. You see, dad and mom took care of my cousins with the six of us during the summers when we were teenagers. My father never went to college but ran his own business. His life and example have remained with me into adulthood.

My first memory of my father was when he came home from work. He would have a little something to eat and take a nap in our family room. Sometimes he would take off his shirt while he napped; he was well built and even had a six-pack. He remained in shape most of his working life, developing a solid physique from working outside in the sun. However, he only stood 5'9".

He worked as an independent contractor pouring concrete for new homes in Florida and was trained as a mason, building concrete foundations, sidewalks, and driveways. His work was extremely strenuous and difficult. After becoming a teenager, I stood taller than my father, but I would never challenge him because of my respect for him and his incredible strength.

My father awoke every morning at 5:00 AM and worked in the Florida heat all year long. The men who worked with him or knew him respected his work ethic.

When I was in middle school, I went to work with my dad to earn money during the summer. I remember being in awe of my dad. One day after arriving at a job site, we got out of the truck where we had to prepare the floor of a house before framing the driveway that was filled with piles of dirt. After we had boarded up the area to set the driveway and sidewalks, the concrete truck came at about 2 o'clock. I think we finished at around five or six o'clock that day, and my dad stopped for 10 minutes to have a sandwich; he worked the entire time. This was during the summer where the weather would typically top out at about 95° or 100°.

My oldest brother, Wendell, took after my dad. He spent his summers working with him pouring concrete while in high school. One day when they were scheduled to pour the foundation for a home in Lakeland, Florida, to the south of town, the truck that delivered sand required to pour the foundation delivered too much. Dad and Wendell were the only men working that day, and Wendell looked at my father and asked, "When are the other men coming to help with this load of dirt?"

"Well, son, looking at the sand is not going to move it - so, let's get going," my dad said.

As they begin to move the mountain of sand in place, dad said, "You have to move it one shovel at a time and use your legs." By 12 noon, they had removed the excess dirt and prepared the foundation for the concrete trucks. My brother told me he would never forget that lesson.

I never heard my father complain, whine, or pout about his life. He loved being responsible and being the breadwinner who provided food, clothing, and shelter while having the energy to engage with his six children after putting in long hours in the sun. When I was one, he and mom purchased the home I grew up in and seemed to be well off supporting us.

My dad supported our goals and dreams. He helped all of us get started with college, although they didn't have a lot of money. Dad and mom never went to college, but they made sure we all had the opportunity to go to college; four out of six of us attended college, and the other two went to vocational schools. They worked hard to support us and made it their goal for us to understand the importance of education.

For the majority of my life growing up, my mom and dad had a great relationship, and she supported him in his efforts to support our family. Like many married couples whose children have left home for college, they experienced their share of marital ups and downs. It was the empty nest syndrome. Mom respected dad because of their relationship and also for the way he supported us.

My parents grew up during the 1930s and 1940s, so being black in the south wasn't a walk in the park. I personally felt like I grew up wealthy and was shielded from the social and political tension of the '60s. Like Rosa Parks, my mother was also told to move to the back of the bus or get off; afterward, my father made sure we always had two cars. I personally had no idea.

The men in my town call my dad W.C.; he was well-known within our community. I learned that my dad wasn't someone to play with because of the way the men respected him in town.

He was drafted and served in the military during the Korean War before most of my siblings and I were born. He would tell us interesting stories of his experience in the Army, but he didn't go to Korea.

In the '70s, my father started playing golf, and I have fond memories of going to golf tournaments with him and my sisters, staying in hotels and meeting new friends. Because of his physique and strength, he became a really good golfer, and upon his death, I learned that he won 18 trophies during his time in the amateur black men's golf league. He taught me to play, and after his death, I inherited his golf clubs. I've learned to play pretty well using his clubs.

One of the most poignant memories I have of my father was the way he worked to take care of his mother. My father loved his mother, and he did whatever was required to support her throughout her life and her transition during death.

He also did a lot to take care of others in our community. He served on a number of boards in the church we attended, and he supported many of the elderly that needed help around their homes. He was also an amazing grandfather.

Finally, I remember dad teaching me how to support and raise my own family, especially how important it is to support my daughter as she becomes a young lady. I remember him when I get up and go to work. I remember him when I pay bills, buy food, and ensure we have proper clothing and shelter because that's what dads do. His example helped me to make a decision not to pursue my career as a professional musician so that I would be there for my wife and kids and not go on the road performing. Reflecting back on my dad, strength means a lot to me and has helped me become the man I am today.

It is his stories that have shaped and impacted my life. They have driven me to have a high work ethic, which, as a musician is essential. There is no short cut to greatness- it takes practice, practice and more practice.

How do stories directly impact your workplace and team? In the next section, I will tell you a story that drove a team to consistent greatness every time we discussed it.

---

15 days till lift-off

In 2014, I started my consulting practice and partnered with a Portfolio Management consulting firm working in the Northern Virginia area. They had won a contract with the State Department of Transportation, and they needed a senior Portfolio Consultant to lead the effort with another developer. They signed a contract with the State Department of Transportation and then had to wait 8 weeks before we had our first meeting, where we quickly learned that we were already behind.

At this meeting, we were tasked to create a solution for an older homegrown system to talk to a Microsoft Project Server 2013 Portfolio application they had purchased for managing over 14,000 projects. We had to create code to allow the two systems to work seamlessly. The problem was we only had 15 days to complete it.

At the first meeting, we determined that we only needed a proof of concept model that could show a demo that the code worked. We also only had to demo for one of a number of systems and projects. While this was a bit of relief, we still only had 15 days before we had to demonstrate it to the CIO who would report our results to the state commissioner.

Every morning our team met, we worked hard as a team to make the miracle happen. And we did it - in 14 days. We had a day to spare. The demo was successful, but more importantly, we had created a story that we could use in the future.

Whenever a new iteration of the program came our way that was challenging, I would remind them how we had tackled the State Department of Transportation proof of concept 15-day deliverable. The story made our team culture more collaborative and more family and results-oriented. The initial 3-month contract has been extended for 2 additional years and counting.

Leveraging a story

There are key elements to a story that have been used in all kinds of mediums.

Freytag Pyramid

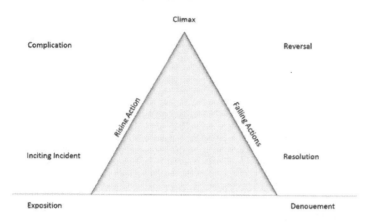

When delivering a story with maximum impact, the elements of the classic Freytag's pyramid can be employed.

Does the story have to belong to have an impact?

Consider many of the moving advertisements you see on television. Many of the most powerful ones have animals, and there is no dialogue. Budweiser commercials often use these stories with their Clydesdale horses as the central characters. Coke used short moving stories for years during the holidays with their polar bear campaigns. Quick, easy to understand, but when inserted into the Freytag's Pyramid, all of the elements are present.

To help leverage your storytelling even further, professional speaker and author, Doug Stevenson, offers nine steps of a story structure:

1. Set the Scene
2. Introduce the Characters (Not necessarily Step 2)
3. Begin the Journey
4. Encounter the Obstacle
5. Overcome the Obstacle
6. Resolve the Story
7. Make the Point

8. Ask "The Question."
9. Repeat the Point / The Phrase That Pays

He uses these steps in his talks when constructing a story, but in your business, unless you are sending out an email, or talking in a formal way in your organization, this may seem a bit difficult to do spontaneously.

Using stories are strategic, and therefore you can prepare your story ahead of time. You can figure out how you want to tell it, and then try to stick to that structure when you deliver it. Throughout this book, you will notice I use many stories, and most of them fit within this structure.

It is important to connect with your audience (whoever is listening) emotionally, but don't get bogged down in the details. Keep the story moving and keep it relevant. That is why I suggest that your best stories are figured out and practiced ahead of time.

With that in mind, allow me to end with a story.

I have played the bass for many years, and most of my early college education had been focused on music and ministry (In this story I am the main character, and now you know a little about me).

Because the music industry is tough to make a living at, I decided to create other streams of income and follow other paths of interest that have led me to where I am today (maybe a little foreshadowing here).

I had forgotten how much I really loved music until recently when I received a call and an email that brought me back to music in a big way. (Setting the scene).

I had played the bass last year during a music set with a band of speakers who were also musicians, as well as with Joey Cook from American Idol, at the 2015 National Speakers Association National Conference in Washington DC. I really loved the experience, but how could I make the shift. (The journey). I am a fulltime consultant and businessman, who has time for music? How could I really do both? (Obstacle).

I was given not one, but two opportunities. The first was an email to invite me to play with the band again at the National Speakers Association Conference. The second was a call about performing in the pit orchestra of a show I had played many years ago. The composer/director wanted to do the show again, but could not think of a bass player that could do both jazz and classical. I was made for the part. (Overcoming the Obstacle).

I became very optimistic that I could live in both worlds, which has helped me with the concept of this book. I was given the opportunity to incorporate what I was really passionate about in my life, with the life and business I had chosen. (Resolving the Story).

Never give up on your passion. Be creative and find ways to incorporate it into your life. For me, not only was I able to perform again, but it helped me transform my business platform and brand into something new and unique. (Making the point).

Now it's your turn, develop a story for your organization or project using the Freytag's pyramid structure. Then share it with a colleague or family member, elicit their feedback and work on improving the story and your delivery of the content.

Questions to Consider

1. What are your best-untold stories?
2. How are you going to tell and live your story? I once heard a speaker say, A Brand is a Story embedded in the mind of the market.
3. How will we inspire attachment and buy-in with our storytelling?
4. What do you want people to think about after you've told your story?

Strategies for Application

1. If you're not an accomplished storyteller, signup for Toastmasters.
2. Volunteer to give presentations at work or in a community organization and record yourself. Ask for feedback, and make course corrections.

3. Watch TED talks to see and learn from great storytellers.

Additional Resources

- The Irresistible Power of Storytelling as a Strategic Business Tool From https://hbr.org/2014/03/the-irresistible-power-of-storytelling-as-a-strategic-business-tool/
- Why Your Brain Loves Good Storytelling From https://hbr.org/2014/10/why-your-brain-loves-good-storytelling/
- Good Companies Are Storytellers. Great Companies Are Storydoers From https://hbr.org/2013/07/good-companies-are-storyteller
- Sunny Leone: It is important to connect with your audience .., http://www.news18.com/news/movies/sunny-leone-it-is-important-to-connect-with-yo (accessed June 24, 2016).
- PofE 025: Father's Day Post: My Father's Work Ethic .., http://www.principlesofexecution.com/principles-of-execution/2012/11/my-fathers- (accessed June 24, 2016).

CHAPTER 6

BEST PRACTICE

"Innovation and best practices can be sown throughout an organization - but only when they fall on fertile ground." Marcus Buckingham

"If you can't explain it simply, you don't understand it well enough." Albert Einstein.

Values are of little importance unless they are enshrined in a company's practices. If an organization professes, "People are our greatest asset," it should also be ready to invest in people in visible ways.

There is the easy way and the right way. The easy way may look inviting, but it may not get you to your destination. When developing a PPM culture, it should always be done with an eye toward best practices.

What are best practices? A simple definition is any method or technique that shows results that are superior to those achieved by other methods, and that is then used as a benchmark.

Why do best practices work, and what can they do for companies?

- Best practices will align with your strategy.
- They help to reduce costs.
- They improve productivity.
- They promote timely execution when utilized correctly.
- They provide for better decision-making.
- They leverage/exploit existing/emerging technologies.
- They can ensure acceptable levels of control and risk management.
- They can be used to optimize the skills and capabilities of the organization.
- Best Practices promote collaboration across the extended enterprise.

Music is an Unforgiving Master

To learn to play an instrument is not hard. I can teach just about anyone to draw a bow across the strings of my bass, and a sound will emit. It is a sound, though, not music. As I began to learn music, I learned the basics of reading notes, clefs, time signatures, and even foreign words to describe the speed or mode of a particular piece. There is no shortcut; you just have to learn these basics to read music.

There are those that don't read music who are phenomenal musicians, but they would not make it in a symphony as reading music is essential.

There's a breaking point that musicians inevitably hit, no matter how much raw talent they have. It's the line between amateur and professional. This is not about being paid; it is a level of proficiency- and there are best practices to achieve the desired goal. There are no shortcuts; no easy roads.

There is learning, practicing, more learning, more practicing, and on and on. In fact, even the best musicians in the world often have teachers; they go back to for lessons. It's about enjoying the journey and becoming the best musician you can become.

I could fill an entire book about what it takes to become a professional musician, but the secret sauce is the practice room. The dreaded small room in which you practice the same music passages over and over again until they become muscle memory.

What differs is how exactly you practice. Do you do scales- do, re, mi, fa, sol, la, si, do? Do you practice etudes- which are repetitive combinations of notes? Do you do long warm-up exercises? Some instruments, such as brass, actually have to warm down. Each instrument has their own best practices, and each teacher has their own set that they instill into their students.

Once, a musician gets to this level of professionalism; there are certain expectations that not only help the musician but the orchestra as a whole.

When you arrive for a rehearsal, it is not good practice to sight-read; that is reading the music for the first time. This is a letdown to your section, the other musicians in the orchestra, the conductor, and ultimately the audience. There is only so much time allotted to practice, and if musicians have not practiced their parts, it takes longer for them to get up to speed and actually begin to make music.

In most any section, unless a musician has a solo, they are expected to blend with the other musicians. The section should sound like one instrument. If a musician has not practiced, they are more prone to make mistakes, which will stick out in an orchestra. That is just one musician. Imagine if some musicians have not practiced. Chaos ensues, and the blood pressure of the conductor will rise- which does not bode well for the musicians.

There is a mission that is set in motion before every concert an orchestra performs - to entertain their audience with the beauty of the music and the proficiency in which it is played. Best practice dictates that this does not occur at the first rehearsal. It occurs the day each musician receives their music.

There is another universal best practice of an orchestra. Arrive on time. When the stick comes down, you had better be seated, prepared, and warmed up. Latecomers are frowned upon, not only by the conductor but by other musicians. Again, it slows down the process and impacts the shared goal.

There is one tool every musician must-have, and if they don't, they better find one quickly — a pencil with an eraser. During practice, lessons and rehearsals pencils are used in music to make notes and to highlight things the musician needs to pay attention to in the music. String players often use pencils to mark when a bow goes up and when it comes down. If you have ever watched an orchestra, there is a kind of choreography that occurs. All the bows in a section are moving in the same direction at the same time.

A rehearsal is a time to make notes given by the conductor. Play softer. Play louder. Play slower. Watch for a cue. Circle a change in key, so you are playing the right notes.

It has to be a pencil with an eraser because when you are done playing, you must be able to erase your notes so that the next musician who reads it has a clean copy. It is common courtesy.

All of these are best practices. Sure you can choose to be chronically late, without a pencil, and look at the music for the first time, but eventually, you may be asked to leave because no one musician is irreplaceable. Best practices equal best performances.

How Companies Leverage Best Practices

Best Practices permeate an entire organization and can be seen in different contexts within a company's culture. Consider the best practices of the companies below.

Google
Google has a process of product development that is informal and allows staff member's access to the co-founders and CEO. This is best practice for two reasons - one it creates a broader field for developing new technologies, and two, everyone in the company feels that they are connected and heard.

Wegmans
Wegmans, a Food market chain, is consistently voted as one of the best places to work in the United States. Their focus is not quick expansion; rather, they only open a few stores every year. One of their best practices is that they send their best employees from the other stores to set up a new location. They make sure the store is set up properly before they open the doors. In addition, they spend millions of dollars training their employees to ensure they are ready to work before the grand opening.

DreamWorks Animation
Best practices can lead to employee retention as evidenced by Dream Works' impressive 97 percent employee retention rate. This can be due to their practice of encouraging employees to take risks and openly communicate their ideas with executives and creating spontaneous creativity sessions.

Salesforce.com
Salesforce.com uses a social networking application called Chatter, within their organization that allows employees to share ideas, analyze data, and even compare drafts of documents in real-time. Having access to real-time data eliminates the lag associated with the use of email and other older methods of communication.

How do you implement Best Practices?

One of the critical components of implementation is communication. As I mentioned earlier, when talking about goals, missions, and other plans, information must be disseminated in a clear and concise way. You need allies that are well informed of what the practices are and why they are important to the organization.

Once key personnel is aware of the best practice, then they must be held accountable for implementing it. It is up to the managers to identify which employees will be responsible for executing the practices. There has to be a plan of accountability that is observable and measurable. It is important to keep everyone accountable for their roles.

A way to ensure accountability is to follow-up. Nothing is worse than creating a practice and not following up to make sure that it is being implemented. Create a plan to assess and evaluate the success of the practices to not only be sure that they are being executed, but that to ensure they are effective.

Best Practices evolve and change over time, and so an organization must keep their eye on the prize and make sure their practices are truly the best and up to date. Organization's need to develop a strategy and specific dates for follow-up ensure that it occurs.

The Eight Steps to Developing Best Practices

1. **Do Your Homework:** What other companies in your industry come to mind when considering best practices? Which ones outside your industry personify best practices? Do research to determine what they do in areas such as hiring, customer service, or anything else that catches your attention. You can do Google searches, read trade magazines, or even ask others in your business whom they respect as a business with solid best practices. You don't have to reinvent the wheel; you can follow the paths of authors and adapt what they have done within your organization.

2.   **Share Your Information:** As mentioned earlier, once you determine what practice you want to begin implementing within your organization, be sure that you are clearly sharing it with key personnel in a clear and concise manner. Emphasize why the best practices matter and how it will benefit them, the organization, and your customers. Send out emails and schedule meetings. Try not to implement too much at once. Prepare your employees and roll out the changes slow enough for people to adapt. This is a critical step; people can only consume what they can digest, so implement changes in small portions.

3. **Define Your Metrics:** Be sure that when you develop your practices, they have measurable metrics for accountability and as an indicator of success. You may have to have a consulting company create these for you. The important thing is that whatever you do, it is measurable. Suppose for instance, that you want to cut the wait time for customers connecting with customer service. A clear best practice would reduce wait time to 5 minutes. If the current average wait time is 7 minutes, then you want to reduce it by 2 minutes. That is measurable. To just say you want customers to wait less time on the phone is not a clear and measurable metric.

4. **Manage Change:** Change is difficult for most people. They often resist it, so be prepared for it, and have a strategy to manage it. Most people resist change. Make sure you have a plan in place to deal with people's fears. This plan should not only look internally but should also look at the resistance to change of your stakeholders and customers. Again there are consulting companies that specialize in change. They can create a forecast for your company about how your employees will deal with change and can mitigate problems before they start with strategic intervention.

5. **Modify and Customize for Your Business:** When considering a best practice, especially one that may be outside your industry, take the time to modify it to work within your organization. Ask for feedback and suggestions (this may be a best practice in itself). Be open and be willing to take risks.

6. **Involve Everyone:** Be sure everyone understands what you are implementing, that they know their role and that they have bought in. Once again, be open to feedback and follow up with everyone.

7. **Align Business and Customer Needs:** Sometimes, it may be necessary to involve another company to help you develop and implement new best practice strategies. Never forget that you know your business best and advocate when you need to. If you do not feel a particular best practice aligns with your company, and the mission, then it may not be the right one. You may need to reject or modify it.

8. **Evaluate and Refine:** Keep in mind best practices sometimes need modification or replacement. The most successful businesses evolve, are prepared for those changes, and are consistently adjusting and aligning their strategy to external and internal changes.

Questions to Consider

1. How can you ensure that the projects you select are aligned with your organization's strategy, goals, objectives, tactics, and resource's capabilities and capacity to deliver the right results?
2. Are you using a data-driven process for how you select where to invest your limited resources?
3. Have you established a consistent project meeting framework to ensure your projects are remaining on target to deliver the benefits and outcomes you and your stakeholders are expecting?
4. Have you developed a process to ensure that the right information is communicated to the right people at the right time to keep everyone informed of your team's progress?

Strategies for Application

1. Identify the best-performing organizations in your industry and find out how they perform in areas you need to improve in.
2. Read 3 books about different organizations that are consistently ranked among the best places to work, and figure out why their people love them so much. Then, find a way to imitate what you've read.

3. Review your current list of projects against your mission, vision, values, goals, and objectives, and determine if they are aligned with your strategic direction.
4. Develop a schedule to engage your key stakeholders and team and elicit their feedback and input. Make it fun.

Additional Resources

- Best Practices in IT Portfolio Management
  http://sloanreview.mit.edu/article/best-practices-in-it-portfolio-management/
- Cultural Change That Sticks
  https://hbr.org/2012/07/cultural-change-that-sticks
- Research: Why Best Practices Don't Translate Across Cultures
  https://hbr.org/2016/06/research-why-best-practices-dont-translate-across-cultures

CHAPTER 7

ENVIRONMENT

Imagine what the people at Disney World feel like every day going to work. They see Cinderella's castle and are reminded that they are at the happiest place on Earth.

The environment we work in affects who we are, what we think, and how we feel. There is a lot of research in this area, and businesses are changing the way they look and feel. I am not talking about the upgrade of a store or restaurant because those are usually for the customers or clients. When I am talking about the environment, I am referring to those that work at a particular organization.

The Concert Hall

Orchestras play in a wide variety of venues, each with its own feel, and sound. We refer to concert halls as being live or dead. By this, we mean whether the sound reverberates or whether it just dies in the first few rows.

Why is the environment important to a musician? We rely on what we hear to make music. Even rock bands have monitors- which are speakers pointed toward the musicians. It gives them a sense of what they sound like. This determines volume, pitch, the blending of instruments, and the musicality of the sound.

The challenge with venues that are too live is that they have an echo effect. Indoor sports arenas and even high school gyms have this issue. They are large and are built of material that reflects sound.

A friend of mine was once at a concert in which a choir of singers was not next to the musicians. The venue was a large convention space. There were 60 musicians, an adult choir of about 90, and school choirs totaling about 150 kids. All of this was supposed to be conducted by one conductor.

There was not a space big enough to rehearse everyone before the day of the concert. In the afternoon, everyone warmed up, and they began to sing and play. It was very obvious that the environment was all wrong. The musicians were not close, nor were they facing the choirs. The result was that the choir was hearing the echo musicians, which was delayed. It was quite a mess.

There was just no room to change the setup, and so the conductor (who was the symphony conductor) conferred with the adult choir and children's choir conductors to come up with a solution.

The problem was syncing the orchestra and choir, so it did not sound like a delay. The other challenge was that the choir could not all clearly see the conductor, so they were relying on what they were hearing.

The solution was two-fold. First, the orchestra was mic'd, and there were monitors placed in front of the choirs.

Each of the choirs had rehearsed with their respective directors prior to the day of the performance. They knew the music, and the choir was used to them conducting. So the second solution was to erect two other podiums side by side to the orchestra conductor. During the performance, they watched the symphony conductor, and they directed their choirs accordingly.

The concert was better than it would have been, but if you have ever been to a sporting event or even a concert in a large space, you know that there is an echo that muddies the sound. Even though everyone was finally playing and singing at the same time now, the sound was bouncing, and it was impossible to understand the words of even the simplest holiday carols.

This was a community event called the Christmas Extravaganza. The idea was to have an annual event. There was no follow-up concert. The environment was not right, and even with solutions for improvement, they could not alter the space.

The opposite problem can occur at a concert. An orchestra can rehearse in a space before a concert, and the hall could sound amazing, and bright. Once the hall is full of bodies, the sound dies. It feels like you are playing in a box lined with sponges.

The sound feels flat, and the emotion uninspired. Some musicians feel like they need to play louder in order to compensate. To the audience, who is hearing the music just fine, some of the musicians sound out of balance because they are overplaying.

Like sports, there is a home-field advantage. Once an orchestra has played in a space many times, they get a feel for it, as does the conductor. They know that the sound will change once there is an audience that will absorb the sound.

How does the environment impact businesses?

A business has to consider the environment in which employees are working. In an orchestra, a hall is evaluated by how it responds to sound. In a business, the consideration is how productive or creative a space is.

For instance, at Pixar, there is a huge open atrium. The idea is that it provides a flow within the company for employees to run into each other throughout the day and interact in informal and unplanned ways.

At Bloomberg News, Michael Bloomberg insisted on a bullpen environment in which journalists interact with one another. He wanted to get away from siloed offices with soundproof doors. What is universal is that environment shapes culture.

Sam Walton, the founder of Walmart, created what has become known as the Wal-Mart Cheer. He came up with the idea after visiting a tennis ball factory in Korea. Each day the employees did a company cheer and morning calisthenics. He really liked the environment this created within the company's culture.

He said, "My feeling is that just because we work so hard, we don't have to go around with long faces all the time - while we're doing all of this work, we like to have a good time. It's sort of a 'whistle while you work' philosophy, and we not only have a heck of a good time with it, we work better because of it."
Here is the cheer the remains the standard even today:

Give me a W!
Give me an A!
Give me an L!
Give me a Squiggly!
Give me an M!
Give me an A!
Give me an R!
Give me a T!
What's that spell?
Wal-Mart!
Who's number one?
The Customer! Always!

A Toxic Environment

A toxic environment is like a bacteria; it catches up with you and could potentially change your core values if you let it. You have to keep the pulse of your organization and make sure that the environment is healthy. Here are five things to watch for:

1. Be sure everyone is communicating clearly and with respect for one another. This is a top-down issue. Pay attention to how employees speak to their supervisors, across departments, with other organizations and even customers. Listen and pay attention to communication patterns. Is there a lack of communication? Is there indirect communication by sending messages to others through a third party? Are people withholding pertinent information? Is the information they are communicating misleading?

2. Are their clear expectations and policies in place within the organization? Does everyone know what they are supposed to be doing? Are they clear on their jobs, roles, and responsibilities? As I have mentioned earlier in the book, this is essential when new policies or ideas are being implemented within an organization. Be sure that expectations and policies are written and clearly understood. This begins from the time a new person is hired, but it must be communicated on a continual basis, especially if there are changes. Without these clear expectations, there can be misunderstandings, bad feelings about the organization and poor quality issues.

3. As we mentioned in a previous chapter, you have to have the right people in the right positions. People can be toxic within an organization, and they can affect the moods, feelings, and even the productivity of those around them. They can have a profound effect on the culture of the entire organization depending on their position. Often toxic leaders think about themselves first, and the best interests of the organization last.

4. The style of communication can also be a factor. Do people seem unhappy, grumpy, and disgruntled when communicating with others? Does this permeate into their communications with customers and others outside the organization? Do people tend to be negative, or are they frowning a lot? There can also be patterns of sarcasm and

cynicism in the way people communicate. All of these can be signs of a toxic underpinning that could grow and also turn people off.

5. A negative and toxic environment can affect people even outside of work. It can affect their physical and mental health. They could have stress-related disorders, insomnia, and it could even affect their weight and put them at risk for more serious health problems. Coming home from a toxic environment can spill over into an employee's personal life, and they can have marital and family problems. They can become irritable and generally unpleasant to be around. It can have cyclical effect in that a person that is unhappy at home can then bring even more negativity back into the workplace.

Using Vision and Purpose

"You can't just give someone a creativity injection. You have to create an environment for curiosity and a way to encourage people and get the best out of them." Ken Robinson

Different musical organizations have a different vision and purpose. For instance, an orchestra often performs in a hall with a large stage. The women dress in black dresses or black pantsuits, and the men dress in tuxedos. All of these create a certain environment.

The audience expects a certain kind of music and experience that is in the character of the orchestra. For instance, a pops symphony would play more popular themed music, but in a classical music style. The audience usually dresses up for these concerts, and a certain feel and expectation of experience occurs. For instance, one would not go in shorts and a t-shirt to an evening symphony performance. It would not match the environment.

A jazz band may play in a larger auditorium, but often they play in a different environment with a different setup and feel. A small jazz combo might set up in a local lounge where the dress code is more casual. There may be talking, eating, and drinking during their performance, which in a symphony setting would be frowned upon. The atmosphere in a jazz performance is much more intimate, and is closer to the listeners, rather than experiencing it far away in the back of a large auditorium. The setting is usually first-come, first-served at whatever tables and booths or even bar stools that are available. Symphony concerts have assigned seats, and the closer you are to the stage, the more the tickets cost. (As an aside, these may not be the best seats to listen to a symphony, depending on the hall. You may have a better auditory experience farther back.)

Be a yardstick of quality.

"Some people aren't used to an environment where excellence is expected." Steve Jobs

The environment of an organization must match the vision and purpose. In the case of Disney, it must feel like the happiest place on Earth. People need to be smiling and friendly, and it must be clean. Could you imagine if the employees were frowning as you go onto a ride? Walt Disney created a workplace atmosphere that was fun and friendly. He demonstrated appreciation and respect towards the workers that brought value to his business.

If you want a creative space, you have to make sure people are around a table or able to think. Confined spaces may confine creativity.

If you need groups of people to brainstorm and come up with new innovative ideas, they should not be in cubicles or closed offices.

The environment of an organization can represent the beliefs of that organization. If the company is behind clean energy, then they may have solar panels on their roof, gardens, and recycling bins. If a company is supportive of families, they may have an onsite daycare and special family leave initiatives.

If health is important, an organization may have an onsite gym, a nurse or nutritionist, or even an exercise program like morning yoga.

Building a Positive Environment

Below are ways that you can begin to build a positive and productive environment within your organization:

1. Encourage Social Connections. When you foster positive social connections between employees, it can improve their health, reduce sick days, help them to recover twice as fast from surgery, experience less depression, learn faster and remember longer, tolerate pain and discomfort better, display more mental acuity, and perform better on the job.

2. Show empathy for your employees and encourage others to do the same within your organization. This fosters trust and goodwill throughout the organization.

3. Find ways to help. It is easy to help people out of a problem or mistake. When we offer help, we then become part of the solution. This promotes goodwill and a feeling that we are in this company together. It creates a sense of community and inclusiveness.

4. Encourage people to share their struggles. While you don't want to be a therapist, you can be seen as caring and empathetic to a person's struggles. They feel that the company cares for them, and they will care in return. As mentioned earlier, Hilton used to sit with his employees every day to talk about their personal struggles and even their triumphs. This practice still exists at individual hotels between management and staff.

5. Create a physically appealing environment. Pay attention to the colors on the walls, and the pictures. Use colors that are bright and patterns that are not cluttered. Moderate complexity in the visual environment is best. Include as few colors as possible.

6. Have people from the outside ask your employees about the environment they work in. This kind of feedback is invaluable. You are looking for consistency and positive remarks. You are also looking for patterns in any negative feedback you receive.

7. Allow your employees to have some control and a say. Get their input about furniture arrangements, lighting, and other aspects of their environment. Also, ask them about other aspects that would make working at the organization more appealing such as daycare, exercise programs, healthy snacks, etc...

Questions to Consider

1. How do you see your work environment?
2. What distinctive elements would you like to see, smell, taste, and hear to make your workplace a representation of your business vision?
3. Does your workplace environment generate the type of atmosphere you need to support the culture you're trying to create?

Strategies for Application

1. Identify top-performing organizations in your industry and benchmark how they operate and set up their work environment.
2. Identify top performers in your own organization and find out what they all do in common, and then teach others to leverage these same processes.
3. Ensure that your tangible and intangible environments are aligned (i.e., Compensation, interesting and challenging work, awards and appreciation events, opportunities for training and advancement, leadership engagement and work/life balance, and flexible scheduling).

Additional Resources

- Is Your Office Culture Toxic? McKinsey Pros Dish On What To Do
  http://www.forbes.com/sites/learnvest/2015/10/22/is-your-office-culture-toxic-mckinsey-pros-dish-on-what-to-do/#110197fb37fc
- Create A Work Environment That Fosters Flow
  https://hbr.org/2014/05/create-a-work-environment-that-fosters-flow/.

CHAPTER 8

EXECUTION

The more constraints one imposes, the more one frees one's self. And the arbitrariness of the constraint serves only to obtain precision of execution. **Igor Stravinsky**

The preparation for a concert really takes years. The symphony will have built a reputation and hired the right conductor and people to perform. The conductor will have practiced and prepared to conduct a large symphony for years and may have worked at other smaller orchestras to build their reputation in order to be noticed and hired as the maestro.

Each musician has spent years practicing and learning the repertoire expected of them to be able to play, not only in an audition but also as a matter of course through their career as a member of the symphony.

The conductor chooses music that reflects the image of the orchestra and music that the audience will sometimes recognize, but they will enjoy no matter what, and music that the musicians are familiar with or that is at least within their ability to perform.

The musicians get the music ahead of time and begin to practice, sometimes for weeks, before the first rehearsal. They may rehearse for a concert 4 or 5 times, and may even have a rehearsal the day of the concert.

Many concerts begin at 8:00 PM, some more on time than others. The musicians are expected to arrive 30 - 45 minutes beforehand. This allows them to warm up, and it allows the personnel to assess that everyone is there and ready to play. If a key player is late, the concert could be delayed, which is really bad. Sometimes weather and other unforeseen circumstances can happen, but the idea is that the show must go on if at all possible. Late is better than never.

If a key player does not make it to a concert, such as a solo oboe player, the concert could be canceled, which is REALLY, REALLY bad. I am lucky in the fact that I belong to the Bass section, so if one player does not show or is late, the show can proceed. A bass player can slip onto the stage between pieces. Depending on the circumstances, it could be their last performance with the symphony.

The concert, which is the symphony's execution, is everything. Without a concert, the symphony will either have to set up a new date, which can be extremely expensive, or money must be returned to the patrons, which could really hurt the symphony's bottom line. If a concert is canceled, in most circumstances, the musicians are paid for just showing up.

Another friend of mine told me about a concert his symphony was going to perform as part of a summer concert series. There was a large storm, and the power was out. All musicians arrived, collected their check at the stage door and went home. The concert was canceled. There was no execution, and even though the musicians were paid, they were disappointed that they did not get to play the concert. Even musicians want to get paid for their hard work. They practice and prepare every day for that moment, the stick goes down, and the music begins. Many of them would live on the applause alone.

Strategy Execution as a Process

The most notable book to date on strategy execution is Execution: The Discipline of Getting Things Done, by Larry Bossidy and Ram Charan. Bossidy. A retired CEO, and (Charan), a renowned management consultant, makes the case for execution as a discipline or as a "systematic way of exposing reality and acting on it." They explain that "the heart of execution lies in three core processes":
1. People
2. Strategy
3. Operations

We have discussed these other processes throughout the book. The execution is the big show. It is what happens when all the elements come together. The more people are aligned and in sync with one another, the better the execution.

There is a group of people at a music performance that is crucial, but you might not see much of, mostly because they move quickly and are dressed in black. This is the stage crew. Without the crew, the musicians would have nowhere to sit, nothing to read music off of, and they would be sitting in the dark.

The backstage crew starts working before the musicians arrive, and often late into the night after the concert is done. They set up the chairs, the bandshell, the stands, the podium, and bring large instruments like pianos on and off the stage. The stage manager sits with a headset backstage and lets the person in the light booth, often in the back of the auditorium, know when to cue the lights, and when the curtain needs to be raised.

In the front of the house, there is the box office manager that makes sure tickets are distributed and sold. Often volunteers help patrons to their seats and give them a program.

There are scores of people that must work together for a performance to happen. Each person has a job, and each manager makes sure that their team is executing their job efficiently, on time and with elegance and grace. They are all a part of the performance, just as much as the conductor and the musicians.

The one thing that can be said with confidence about people involved with a symphony performance is that they want to be there. They want to do their part because they want the execution to be memorable for everyone. They are passionate about what they do, and support the vision of the symphony - they are there to entertain, inspire, and move an audience through music.

Southwest Airlines

Success doesn't necessarily come from breakthrough innovation but from flawless execution. A great strategy alone won't win a game or a battle; the win comes from basic blocking and tackling. Naveen Jain

The purpose of a plane is to get you from point A to point B. There are many airlines you can choose from, and the basic execution is the same. You buy your ticket, you pack your bags, you check your bags, you wait hours in the TSA line, you board the plane, and you sit hoping the stranger sitting next to you for the next four hours is not a salesperson. You fly, you land, you grab your bags, and you are done, as is the airline's obligation to you.

Most airlines offer a "better" option for those who want to pay. They offer a more pleasant flight with extras that will make the experience more enjoyable. They execute the first-class service for their first-class passengers.

There has been one airline, that decided to shake up the entire way people fly. They decided they could tweak the execution and make a new kind of experience. This has been the premise of Southwest Airlines.

First, they got rid of first class. They made the flight more affordable and stopped the game of charging different amounts, sometimes in the hundreds of dollars, based on which seat the person was sitting in. After all, the goal of every flight is to get from point A to point B. Everyone leaves and arrives at the same time, so everyone is equal.

With the idea that everyone is essentially trapped in a metal tube flying at high speeds through open air, they decided to make the flight more fun. Their motto is that they keep the planes in the air and have more fun doing it. It starts with what might be the same boring demonstration about how to use a seatbelt. They flipped the script, adding jokes and made it fun. During the flight, the attendants are jovial and playful, as they have more time to do so. They are not serving meals, only snacks, and cocktails. They are the real entertainment.

Because they have changed the way they execute, Southwest Airlines has become one of the most profitable airlines around.

---

10 Steps to Strategic Execution

Step 1: Create a Vision

The first step in this book was creating a vision, so by now, you should have practice. The difference here is that you will visualize the outcome of your execution. Before a performance, you will often see musicians fingering their instruments, but not making any real sounds. They are visualizing in their head what it will sound like when they are playing their part in the performance. They are making sure they are ready to play the right notes at the right time. They may even play their parts out loud, and the effect with an orchestra "warming up." Everyone is preparing for the performance and playing different parts all at the same time. Once the concertmaster stands up, everyone stops and listens for the tuning note from the oboe. The execution of the performance is about to begin. Everyone knows their role during this period of tuning, even the audience- everyone is quiet and listens and then begins tuning their instrument.

You need to have a clear understanding of what your strategy of execution is. It must be clear, measurable, and doable.

Step 2: Take a measurement of your strategy.

During a rehearsal, the conductor must listen and determine when an orchestra is ready to perform a piece flawlessly. They will rehearse sections over and over until it is just right. If it does not sound right during a rehearsal, then it is likely that it will not be right for the performance. Often the "dress" rehearsal, or the rehearsal prior to the performance, has two purposes. First, it is used for checking the sound of the hall. Many times the dress rehearsal is the first time an orchestra gets to play in a particular hall. They must get used to acoustics and sound. The conductor must adjust their conducting to compensate for the best sounding and balanced performance. The second goal is to just go over those trouble spots one last time to make sure they are ready for the performance. It is rare that the symphony will play the whole concert through at a dress rehearsal.

Measure how your strategy of execution will work, and areas you need to work on. Later in this chapter, you will learn about the ADeXI Framework that contains assessments to assure your strategy is on track.

Step 3: Review your progress.

After the performance, a conductor will often listen to a recording to assess how well the concert sounded and to make notes about weak points in the orchestra. This allows the conductor to be prepared for the next concert. Maybe the symphony needs more rehearsals? Maybe they need the music sooner to practice? Maybe the music was too difficult to execute with so many unseasoned players? The point is to assess the strategy to make sure it does not need changes and adjustments.

Step 4: Identify your strategic projects.

As I have pointed out earlier in the book, there are many projects going on within a symphony at any time. The idea of PPM is that all of these projects need to be identified and categorized. There may be projects going on that are related to strategic execution, such as finding new venues, artists, and musicians for the next season.

Step 6: Synchronize your strategic projects.

Once you have identified the projects, you must then make sure they are aligned with the vision and other components of the organization. For instance, you would not seek out musicians that only played pop music for a symphony that primarily played Mozart. You can improve the overall operations, find the right people, and therefore create a more successful strategic execution in all the areas and projects within an organization.

Step 7: Focus on streamlining your project management processes

To successfully execute strategies within an organization, there needs to be a strong project management framework in place. There has to be oversight on projects, or they will not reach their goals on time and /or with the outcomes that were set for them.

A sectional rehearsal is a great time for musicians to bond within a section. It is a time to reconnect and even socialize, but the goal is that the section is rehearsing and preparing their parts in order to be ready for the next full rehearsal. If there is no oversight and strong project management, then the socialization could become the focus, and the outcome will not be achieved.

Step 8: Communicate Expectations

There has to be a strong communication of what the execution strategy is. We have explored this earlier. There has to be a clear understanding from the top down of what the strategy will be, how it will be executed, and who will be responsible. The leaders must be able to communicate the vision, or the strategy will fall apart.

Consider the sectional rehearsal. Usually, these are run by the section leader. Suppose there is a big performance with three large pieces to be performed. The next full rehearsal will concentrate on the Violin Concerto. If the conductor does not communicate the focus of the rehearsal and therefore would need to be the focus of the sectional, then there could be a problem. The section leader may decide that the section needs to work on the Overture piece, and they spend the next three hours on it. Once they return to the rehearsal, the conductor becomes angry because the section is spending a lot of time writing in bowings and notes in their scores. To the conductor, they are not prepared, and would often blame the section leader.

This kind of communication breakdown should be avoided, and so time has to be spent not only describing the strategy but also making sure it is understood who will be responsible for its execution.

Step 10: Reward performance.
For an orchestra, the reward of a well-executed performance is quite evident at the end. The audience is on their feet, clapping vigorously, and yelling, "Bravo." To a musician, this is the greatest reward. Receiving money for it is merely compensation; it is not a reward. After a performance, the audience and the musicians often mingle. Musicians love to hear how great the performance was executed. This is their reward.

It has to be clear what a reward is and what is compensation for a job. A salary is not a reward, but a financial bonus is. A reward does not always have to be monetary - it can be a party, a card, a note taped to a desk, or a public thank you. This part cannot be missed or understated.

If a musician, who is like any other worker in a corporation, never receives their standing ovation, they will either quit the organization and find a better one or quit performing altogether. If they stay and do not feel appreciated or re-warded, they can bring down morale and affect everyone around them.

A standing ovation costs an audience nothing, but they know it is the best way they can show their appreciation for a job well done. It is up to the leaders of an organization to figure out what a standing ovation looks like for their employees.

The ADeXi Framework ™

The ADeXI Framework™ is a systematic process I've developed to help my clients consistently and repeatedly assess, design, execute and improve a best in class project portfolio management processes, and to make the most of their constrained resources and budgets. The framework is based on my 20+ years of experience in project portfolio management and is aligned with industry best practices. The framework is based on what I have observed that works in the real world, and what does not. I've attempted to include in the framework only elements that I have experienced that have had a marked improvement on my clients, and I've removed any unnecessary processes and tools that have not added value. Below is an outline of the framework.

- Assess - Assessing an organization's capability in project portfolio management requires a systematic framework that you can use to define the nature of your organization's project management processes;

an approach, which is objective and allows comparisons both within and across industries is required. This step focuses on:

- o Conduct a PPM Maturity Assessment - use the web link below to take a free PMO 360 Assessment https://principlesofexecution.nsvey.net/ns/n/PMO360.aspx
- o Conduct a Gap Analysis
- o Identify Actions to Close Gap
- o Develop a roadmap to prioritize actions and create a way forward

- Design – Designing the Project Portfolio Management process step helps an organization determine the approach to create, develop, or improve policies, processes, and procedures that enable change. This step ensures that the organization is change ready, and will implement a PPM process that is aligned with the organization's strategic vision, values, and mission. This step focuses on:
  - o Creating a Portfolio Strategic Plan
  - o Developing a Portfolio Charter
  - o Creating a Portfolio Roadmap
  - o Developing a Portfolio Management Plan
  - o Creating the Portfolio (Technical, Process, and HR Solutions)
  - o Validating the organization's Program and Project Management Methodologies
  - o Developing a 4 prong approach to Project Portfolio Management Training across the organization
  - o Executive Level
  - o Functional and Line Manager Level
  - o PMO, Program and Project Manager Level
  - o Business and Technical Team Member Level

- Execute – Executing the Project Portfolio happens at the organizational level, and requires a senior-level executive to sponsor or champion the implementation effort. Enacting this change is a major organizational project, and requires the first 6 principles for developing a culture that works to have been developed and established. This step focuses on:
  - o Implementing the Project Portfolio Management design in increments the organization can absorb. No big bang approaches; they don't work.
  - o Implementing a technical environment My Favorite tools:

- o Microsoft Project Portfolio Server
- o Transparent Choice Portfolio Prioritization Solution
- o Implementing a robust communication strategy
- o Communicating the Portfolio through SMART Portfolio Reports
- o Implementing a Portfolio Review Board and Oversight Committees using the RACI Chart model
- o Implementing and streamline the organization's Governance Boards and Oversight Procedures
- o Establishing a re-calibration process to align the portfolio with the organization's strategy
- Improve – Improving the PPM process is like flying a commercial airliner. Once you take off, you are continuously and consistently adjusting and aligning the flight to reach your destination. Without continuous improvement, your initial efforts to implement a PPM process will eventually fail. Continuous improvement is a critical part of the PPM process. This step focuses on:
  - o Soliciting feedback on portfolio performance and process improvements
  - o Conducting additional PPM Assessments to target the next level of maturity model improvements
  - o Monitoring and measuring portfolio performance
  - o Updating the portfolio processes to improve performance
  - o Training, mentoring and coaching the portfolio management and executive team
  - o http://www.principlesofexecution.com/principles-of-execution/project-portfolio-management-training.html

---

Questions to Consider

1. How do you motivate yourself to perform at your best consistently?
2. How do you motivate your organization or team?
3. How do you keep up with the latest techniques and practices for being effective and efficient with your time while delivering great results?
4. What are you doing to get better in your critical skills every day? Excellence is a habit which can be improved with daily practice.

Strategies for Application

1. Establish a cadence of weekly team meetings to help the team members hold each other accountable for achieving results.
2. Create clearly defined levels of authority and decision-making process to streamline activities within your organization. Build a RACI chart for your most critical process.
3. Establish systems that display the right information to the right people at the right time for effective information flow.
4. Establish intangible motivators that will keep everyone excited and inspired to give their best.
5. Develop a detailed plan for change and transition management. When change happens, most organizations struggle with the transition to the new change environment, which takes a longer time to adopt.

CHAPTER 9

11 MOST COMMON MIS-TAKES, OR HOW NOT TO DE-VELOP A CULTURE THAT WORKS.

A re you ready to start playing bass in a symphony? Maybe not, but you should have the tools to create a culture that works. Here are the principles once again.

1. Vision - Creating a unified vision for your organization.
2. Values - What are the values that represent the organization, both internally and externally?
3. Buy-in - People must be engaged and support the vision and values of a company.
4. Stories - What is the underlying story of the organization that is shared and used to motivate employees?
5. Best Practices - The organization adheres to the highest standards in everything they do.
6. Environment - Where do people work, and under what conditions-physically, mentally, and emotionally.
7. Execution - Once the other six principles are established, it is time to create and implement an execution strategy.

It is easy to just tell you to follow the principles, and you will develop a great culture, but that would not be fair. Even in the best of circumstances, there are some pitfalls and mistakes people make. Below I have listed the top 11 common mistakes that companies make when approaching PPM development.

1.   Taking the wrong approach to creating buy-in and engaging the workforce.

Remember earlier in the book; we discussed the third principle of buy-in. It is not something that is forced; it is something that grows over time. The essential piece is clear communication. From the top-down, the values and the vision must be shared with absolute clarity, and there has to be a definitive- Why. The people within the organization must know why the vision and values are important to them, and the company as a whole. There must be a mechanism of feedback and inclusion. When people feel they are being heard and are part of the process, they will have greater buy-in. Don't simply listen to ideas; you must also try to implement and test them.

If an orchestra conductor does not have buy-in from the players, it will affect everything they do, all the way to the performance. They will follow the conductor, but they have to have bought in and respect the conductor's vision to have maximum execution.

2.   Poor or no plan to implement the desired culture.

You have taken the first steps by reading this book to begin developing an execution strategy. It is not effective to tell people what needs to happen within a team or organization without developing the plan of execution. This may seem like an obvious misstep, but it is often missed. You can have all of the other principles in place, but without a plan in place, they are nothing but some good ideas that never make their way from the whiteboard to reality.

If there is a new dress code for the symphony, there has to be a plan for how that information will get to the symphony members. They could mail out notices to all the players. They could have multiple announcements at rehearsals, and they may even have people model the new dress code. If a paper is just thrown on a stand with a note about a new dress code, there is no way of knowing whether everyone received one, or if they did receive one did they read it, or if they read it did they understand it. It could be a disaster on concert night if only half of the orchestra would be wearing the new dress code outfit and the other wearing the original black outfit.

3.   Getting your staff's input, but not following through on any recommendations.

It is important to open the door to feedback and input, but there has to be follow-through. You don't have to try and implement everything suggested, but you should at least communicate with those that contribute and entice them to continue. Put a value on participation and innovation. This creates new ideas and buy-in.

There are often orchestra committees that are formed within symphonies that meet and listen to concerns and proposed changes for the orchestra. There may be one representative that then takes those concerns to the conductor. If the conductor does not respond or never accepts any of the suggestions, then the committee will not have any purpose, and this could have a negative effect on the rest of the orchestra.

4.   Too many directions from the top

You have to trust people down the chain of command. Nobody enjoys being micromanaged. There is also an issue of trust by allowing people to create their own processes to get the job done. It may not be your process, but the outcome is what is important. You have to trust those you give responsibilities to make decisions and lead those they are hired to lead.

It does not make sense for a conductor to be a part of a sectional rehearsal. They may give input and directions to the section leaders, but they have to rely on those leaders to rehearse the section.

5.   Not aligning culture changes with the organization's strategy and goals

There is nothing more confusing than implementing a change that is not in alignment with the company's vision and values. For instance, if a company decides that family is important, and then implements mandatory weekend overtime work because they are falling behind on their numbers, this becomes paradoxical.

If one of the visions of an orchestra is to play more concerts at area schools but instead add more chamber music concerts, this would seem to be a contradiction.

6.   Lack of clear Roles and Responsibility

It can be frustrating for everyone when someone does not know what their roles and responsibilities are. The question is who is responsible for teaching people what their roles are and what the expectations are. It may be easier to judge and point out when someone drops the ball, but it is much more helpful to be sure they understand what their position is, who relies on them, what others expect of them and when. This is especially important when changes are handed down to be implemented. Clear communication about who is responsible for implementing those new changes is essential.

If the concertmaster (first chair violin) is expected to stand, and cue the oboe to play three tuning notes, then both the concertmaster and the oboe player have to be clear about their roles and expectations. If at the beginning of a concert, a concertmaster stood, and nothing happened, it could create an immediate awkward silence. If the oboe only played one tuning note, then two-thirds of the symphony would not have tuned.

7.   Leadership being inconsistent or Leadership, not setting an example of being the change they seek to make.

It does not work to have a "do as I say, not as I do," philosophy. In an orchestra, there is an expectation that the players are warmed up, they have all their music, they have practiced and that they have a pencil ready. If a conductor walks in without a baton, they forgot their music in their office, or they seemed confused in their conducting, they will lose the respect of the players, and their buy-in to what the conductor would want to accomplish.

8.   Taking on too much change or lack of capacity to absorb the change

You have to change incrementally, rather than all at once. If you try too much, too soon, it will frustrate people and has the potential of failure.

A few years ago, a friend's symphony decided that they needed to increase the musicianship of the orchestra. There were many people past their playing prime, and there were a lot of young, inexperienced players that were just filling slots as extra musicians rather than contract musicians. The difference was that an extra is hired as a warm body, whereas a contract musician has to audition.

They held auditions for the open positions, and so those extras could audition, but they would be in competition with other competent players. This could have been a first good step in raising the musicianship of the orchestra, but they took one step beyond that. The conductor decided to re-audition everyone in the orchestra. This could mean a musician who had been in the orchestra for years could be pushed out, and whole sections could be rearranged. Many musicians quit, and for the next couple of seasons, the morale and cohesiveness of the orchestra had to be rebuilt. It was too much change all at once.

9.   Not protecting your critical resources and people from the impact of too much change at once.

This is related closely to number 8. In the example, key musicians either quit or did not audition well or were demoted in the section. This might seem the best way to improve the orchestra, but it actually hurt them. Nobody felt safe, people felt betrayed, and the community (audience) was even drawn in because they had connections to the many of the long-standing musicians. Tickets sales went down, and season ticket holders did not renew.

It may have been more prudent to make some minor changes in the sections incrementally over time. Also, they needed to honor the longevity of the musicians, some of whom had played with the organization for 30 or more years.

Can you imagine working in a job and then all of a sudden you had to reapply for your own position against other people? How would you feel? Before organizations implement change, they need to decide how much, and over what period of time would have the least negative impact.

10. Not connecting emotionally with the team to help them navigate the change.

There has to be some level of empathy and rapport with your team. In the case of the symphony example above, there was little consideration of what a huge change re-auditioning would be. Auditions are the most stressful thing a musician must endure. Once they are in a symphony, they never expect to have to do it again. In addition, some of the older musicians found themselves unemployed. The ability to start over in a new symphony is hard. There are not many positions open, and everyone is trying for them. There has to be a sense of how a change will affect people's lives both within and outside the organization. Will a change mean more hours in the office? How could that impact a person's family?

There is the risk of some vulnerability that comes with being emotionally in touch with your employees. The reward is greater buy-in, support, and loyalty. It is all about trust.

11. Poor stakeholder engagement and communication about the change throughout the transition process.

While you don't want to be overly involved or micromanage change, you don't want to be missing in action either. You have to be able to assess whether changes are working, how people are feeling about the change, how people are implementing the change, and what the outcomes are. In the last chapter, I presented you a system of assessment for your execution strategy.

You don't want to just wind up the top, pull the string and let it go. You must see where it goes and pull obstacles out of the way and help change the direction when needed.

Symphonies sometimes put surveys in their programs. This allows the audience to give feedback about the music played, the program for future concerts, and their overall experience. If a symphony decides to add more contemporary music to their performances, it is good to know whether the audience is enjoying it or not.

Well, this brings us to the end of our journey! My goal in writing this book is to provide an interesting and hopefully unique way of thinking about a topic that I love, but which can be very boring. Even if you're not a professional musician, your love for music or your past experiences as a high school or college musician has helped make this book an enjoyable read, and I hope that you've learned a few things along the way. Until next time, go ahead, turn up the bass on your favorite music device and in your organization, and enjoy those low tones that move your heart and that rattle your soul. Culture is foundational, fundamental, and it generates the invisible bond that holds us together. Culture is the bass!

CHAPTER 10

NEXT STEPS

I f you're interested in learning more about Creating A Culture of Execution and the fundamental principles of Project Portfolio Management, I've developed an online program that is complementary to this book. To access my E-Learning Course's website click here: https://geraldjleonard.com/creating-a-culture-of-execution

Creating A Culture of Execution: 7 Steps to Overcoming Team Resistance and Accomplishing More Every day!

Discover the secret for taking your workplace culture from toxic stress to executing its best.

Learn the secret to increasing team productivity that generates real bottom-line results.

Are you a director, project manager, or an agile team member who wants to develop strategies, tips, and techniques to overcome the invisible forms of resistance that causes your projects and culture to fail?

Are you ready to discover how to create a culture of execution in your rapidly changing world?

Does this sound familiar?

Your best people are leaving because they are frustrated with the work environment.

You struggle with misalignment of culture change with the organization's strategy and goals.

You are frustrated by conflicting priorities from upper management.

You are feeling overwhelmed by all the tasks that keep getting put on your plate, but nothing is being taken off.

What if...

You could create a culture shift that makes your organization more effective and productive.

You had a clear step-by-step process to ensure your vision, values, and culture are repeatable, and your customer comes to expect outstanding services each and every time.

Your team can embrace your culture and have the capacity to handle culture changes when they happen without burning out.

If so, join us to...

Learn how to create an engaged workforce to increase productivity, transparency, and communication. Get Team Buy-In like a Championship Sports Team that generates real bottom-line results.

Creating A Culture of Execution: 7 Steps to Overcoming Team Resistance and Accomplishing More Every day!

By the end of this 8 modules / 12-week program, you will discover...

The 3 invisible forms of resistance that causes the greatest culture challenge.

A 7-step framework for establishing a working culture in any organization.

How to create a shared vision and cascade the vision throughout your organization to foster transparency and increase productivity

A practical process to craft a set of values that are behavior-driven and measurable enabling you're allowing for faster hiring, and operational decisions

How to create team buy-in that sticks.

The brain science of conversations and how it impacts relationships and culture.

The impact of stories so you can better connect with your listener's head, heart, and hands.

How to bake best practices into your organization's processes, so they become second nature.

How to create a physical and virtual environment that shapes and reinforces the culture you want

The 4 key tools all teams need to execute on their goals effectively.

Also, this program provides 16 hours of hands-on learning and counts for Professional Development Units (PDUs) or Continuing Education Units (CEUs)

Self Study PDUs 8 CEUs 8

Self Study with weekly Coaching PDUs 16 CEUs 16

To access my E-Learning Course's website click here: https://geraldjleonard.com/creating-a-culture-of-execution

ABOUT THE AUTHOR

Gerald J. Leonard is currently the President, & CEO of Principles of Execution (PofE), a Strategic Project Portfolio Management and IT Governance consulting practice based in the Metro Washington, DC, area. He attended Central State University in Ohio where he received his Bachelor in Music degree and later earned a Masters in Music for classical bass from the Cincinnati Conservatory of Music. After graduation, Gerald moved to New York City, where he worked as a professional bassist and studied with the late David Walters, distinguished professor of double bass at both the Juilliard and Manhattan schools of music.

While living in Manhattan Gerald worked as a full-time minister for the New York City Church of Christ and managed time to fulfill numerous music engagements. After resigning from his ministry position, he was able to devote more time to his music career and spend more quality time with his family.

Several years later Gerald began his Information Technology career, focusing initially on network computing and project management. During the last 20+ years, he has worked as an IT Project Management consultant and earned his

PfMP, PMP, MCSE, MCTS, CQIA, COBIT Foundation, and ITIL Foundation certifications. He has also acquired certifications in Project Management and Business Intelligence from the University of California, Berkeley, Theory of Constraints Portfolio Management Technical Expert from the Goldratt Institute, Hoshin Kanri Strategic Planning, Executive Leadership Certification from Cornell University and The Wharton School: Entrepreneurship Acceleration Program.

In his leisure time, Gerald loves playing golf, travel internationally, and playing his upright bass on special occasions.

HOW TO CONTACT GERALD

I f you're interested in improving your organization's ability to deliver the Right Projects the Right Way, increase Performance and Profits and Grow your People to deliver a better Customer Experience and Results. Gerald can help with his signature keynote, workshops, and training.

E-mail: gerald@principlesofexecution.com

Office: (443) 832-3486

Website: http://www.developingaculturethatworks.com

Sign-up for Gerald Leonards' email newsletter at www.principlesofexecution.com

To purchase bulk copies of this book at a discount for your organization or clients, please contact Principles of Execution, LLC:

gerald@principlesofexecution.com

WANT TO GO TO THE NEXT LEVEL?

"I have no doubt that anyone taking Leonard's Portfolio Management course will receive a huge benefit. The material is organized logically and sequenced in a way that compels understanding and learning throughout. The concepts are presented with clarity and precision. Tools for decision making and managing are imbedded in all aspects of Portfolio Management. No one involved in managing a portfolio of projects should miss the opportunity to learn from an expert."

Gerald Kendall, PMP, Author, Advanced Project Portfolio Management, & the PMO."

"Gerald Leonard has taken a bold first step into an area long neglected. He breaks portfolio management down into manageable chunks and brings clarity to a practice the desperately needs it. Gerald's work examines the totality of portfolio perspectives, from the executive suite to the project manager, and acknowledges the roles of the disparate players across the enterprise. His materials thoughtfully examine not only the theory of portfolio management but also the practical day-to-day of ensuring consistency of strategy and approach.; definitely worth your consideration."

Carl Pritchard, PMP, PMI-RMP, EVP, author of 7 Project Management texts, and the U.S. Correspondent for Project Manager Today (UK).

What Do You Think About This Book?

Here's an opportunity to let me know what you think about this book. You may potentially become a contributor in the next edition of Culture is the Bass. Please complete the following questions below with your complete answers by providing me with what you did, what results in you achieved and how you did it. If I include your feedback or input into the next edition or another book, you will receive a personally signed free copy for your collection.

What strategy did you apply, please provide chapter _____ and page _____?

This is what I did:

These are my results:

This is how I achieved my results:

I am providing my consent to use the above statements as you wish.

Your   signature:

_____

Today's   date:

_____

Copy this page and email me a copy to: gerald@principlesofexecution.com